EASY TO MAKE
PAPERCRAFTS

Pauline Butler

Series consultant: Eve Harlow

ANAYA PUBLISHERS LTD LONDON

First published in Great Britain in 1992
by Anaya Publishers Ltd, Strode House, 44–50 Osnaburgh Street,
London NW1 3ND

Reprinted 1993

Editor Eve Harlow
Design by Design 23
Photography Di Lewis
Illustrations by Cilla Eurich
Artwork by Design 23

British Library Cataloguing in Publication Data

Butler, Pauline
Easy to make papercrafts. – (Easy to make series)
I. Title II. Series
745.54
ISBN 1 85470-033-2

Typeset by Servis Filmsetting Ltd, Manchester, UK
Colour Reproduction by Columbia Offset, Singapore
Produced by Mandarin Offset.
Printed and bound in Hong Kong.

CONTENTS

Introduction

Paper is an inspiring and versatile material, readily available and just waiting to be made into something decorative and useful.

Paper has such creative potential – it is one of the most pleasing materials to work with, it is there in abundance and it is surprisingly adaptable. We take paper in all its forms very much for granted, putting it to use everyday in vast quantities – in the home and at work, with applications as diverse as packaging and insulation to providing books and banknotes. We also value it for its decorative and luxurious uses, colouring and printing it with patterns for the walls of our homes and to lavishly wrap our gifts. We write, draw and paint on it, and sometimes admire it simply for its own sake.

The present awareness of the need to conserve our natural materials has made us re-evaluate paper and become more conscious of what it is, and how we use it.

Paper is basically a mix of cellulose fibres obtained from trees, plants and old rags – any of these materials can be used. The raw fibrous matter is soaked and mashed to a pulp, then processed by hand or machine to become paper sheets. The original process for making paper pulp – much the same as is used today – was first developed in China almost 2000 years ago. It was considered an economical alternative to more costly paper making processes and materials, which usually included silk.

There is renewed interest in paper making, and decorative handmade papers are becoming increasingly popular for making sophisticated goods and stationery. The growing interest in these papers, together with an appreciation of recycled paper – both aesthetically and from a practical point of view – has offered even more opportunities for creating attractive papercraft products.

About this book
In this book I have attempted to assemble a collection of papercrafts to appeal to all interests and ages. You will find the book is divided into chapters to describe the contents, rather than the actual craft skills used in each one, so examples of ever-popular crafts like papier mâché and découpage are found in several chapters. For instance papier mâché is used to make a picture frame and the decorative bowls in the Home Decor chapter, earrings, brooches and bangles in the Jewellery chapter, and the joke fruit in the Toys and

Origami chapter. Découpage appears in Home Decor to embellish candlesticks and ornaments and to cover a tray, while 3D découpage, a variation of the basic technique, is used to create gift cards in the Greetings chapter. Other crafts in the book include paper weaving and basket making, paper lace and frieze cutting as well as flowermaking and the Japanese art of paper folding – origami. In the Stationery chapter you will discover how to make desk accessories that look as good as the ones you buy in shops but will cost a fraction of the price! The same applies to the Greetings chapter where you can see how to make a selection of gift packaging and greetings cards.

Making a start
Before you make a start on any of the design ideas, read the Better Papercrafts chapter as all the methods used in the projects are described here in detail. Basic tools and equipment are described and you will also find useful advice about choosing and handling different types of paper as well as folding, cutting, tearing and gluing it. This chapter also tells you how to achieve a professional standard of finish, which can make so much difference to the look of a design that you will be proud of it, however lacking in experience or confidence you may be. Many of the projects, like the rolled paper beads, woven tote bags and papier mâché jewellery, bowls and fruit are simple enough for children to make, and the decoration and colour choices can always be changed to appeal to younger tastes. Other projects can be made by

children with a little adult help and supervision, especially when using sharp scissors, spray adhesive or assembling any awkward bits. However, from a practical point of view, tasks that use potentially dangerous tools like a craft knife or scalpel, or require a degree of strength and precision – like cutting thick card, using Superglue or oil based paints and varnish – should be reserved for adults.

It is a good idea to start a collection of paper bits and pieces – such as glossy magazines, packaging, gift wrappings, cards and trimmings – you might well find a use for them sooner than you think!

Home office

Choose vibrant colours and patterns to make cheerful stationery storage. This set comprises a useful concertina file, a mini chest of drawers and a pencil tub.

CONCERTINA FILE
Materials
Strong thick card
Giftwrap paper laminated to cartridge paper
Three sheets of Canson (art paper)
1yd (90cm) of grosgrain ribbon, 1in (2.5cm) wide
Self-adhesive plastic
Spray adhesive; clear craft glue
Masking tape

Making the file
1 From thick card cut two 13 × 10in (33 × 25cm) rectangles. Cut a card strip for the spine, 13 × 3¼in (33 × 8cm). Spray the laminated gift paper with adhesive on the cartridge side and cover the card using the folded corner technique (page 102).

2 Cut a strip of cartridge paper 13 × 3in (33 × 8cm) and a strip of plastic 13 × 5in (33 × 12.5cm). Peel off the plastic backing paper and apply the cartridge centrally. Position this across the wrong side of the covered card rectangles to make the spine lining.

3 Cut another strip of plastic, 16 × 4½in (41 × 11cm). Hang the folder, right side out, over the edge of the table. Gradually peel the backing paper from the plastic and stick ½in (12mm) on to the edge of the folder. Smooth over the spine. Turn the folder over and continuing to peel the backing paper, smooth the plastic on to the other edge. Fold the short ends over to the inside and press flat.

4 **Ties:** Cut two 18in (45cm) lengths of ribbon. Mark the position for these 1¼in

(3cm) down from the middle of the long edges on the right sides of the folder. Use a craft knife to cut slits the exact width of the ribbons. Push the ribbon ends

Position the plastic-covered cartridge paper on the two card rectangles

Hang the folder over the table edge, apply the self-adhesive plastic to the spine

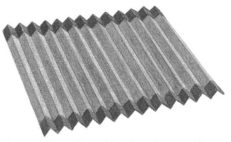

Cover the long edges of the pleated paper with strips of self-adhesive plastic

through the slits to the wrong side. Secure on the other side with a dab of clear glue and leave to dry. Cover the ribbon ends with masking tape.

5 Linings: Cut two pieces of Canson paper $12\frac{3}{4} \times 9\frac{1}{2}$in (32.5 × 24cm) to line the inside covers. Spray with adhesive and press in place.

6 Concertina sides: Make the pleated sides from two strips of Canson paper, each 13 × 8½in (33 × 21.5cm). Mark into ½in (12mm) concertina pleats (see pages 104) and fold into shape. Open the pleats and cover the long edges with 13 × 2in (33 × 5cm) plastic strips folded in half over the pleat edges. Re-press the pleats sharply.

7 Dividers: From Canson paper cut ten 12 × 6¼in (30 × 16cm) rectangles. Edge each with folded plastic strips.

8 Run a line of adhesive down the divider sides and starting 2 pleats in, position the first divider into its pleat with the top edge of the divider level with the lower edge of the sticky plastic edging on the pleat. When all ten dividers are in position, pinch the pleats tightly together and leave the folder under a weight to form its shape.

Finishing

9 To join the pleated file section to the folder, open the folder and position the pleats centrally across the spine. Run adhesive down the end of the pleats at one end of the folder section and press to the inside cover. Press firmly to stick. Repeat at the other end of folder section making sure the pleats are aligned on both inside covers. Press to stick, and leave under a weight, closed, until dry.

Draw the chest shape from this diagram

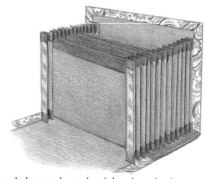

Spread glue on the ends of the pleated sides, press to the inside cover

MINI CHEST OF DRAWERS
Materials
Thick card for the chest, medium-weight card for the drawers
A sheet of giftwrap paper laminated to cartridge paper
Self-adhesive plastic (or contrast paper) for linings
Three small handles, optional
Spray adhesive, clear craft glue, gummed paper tape
Gold paint, optional

Making the chest
1 Draw the shape from the diagram on to thick card and cut out. Score along the fold lines. Fold, then join, the edges by running adhesive down the sides. Press to stick, then reinforce the joins with strips of gummed paper tape, with an overlap to the inside.

Measure round the chest for the paper length, add overlap. Measure the depth of chest and add overlap on front and back edges

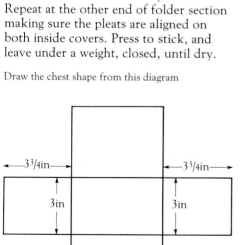

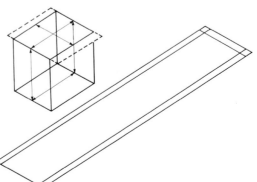

2 To make the drawer dividers measure the inside depth and width and cut two pieces of card to this size. To mark the positions for these, divide the inside depth of chest into three. Run glue along the side edges of the dividers and stick in place. Reinforce the joins with strips of folded gummed tape.

3 **Covering the chest:** Measure round the top sides and base of the chest and draw a rectangle this size by the depth on giftwrap paper. Add an extra $\frac{1}{2}$in (12mm) to the end for overlap. Add $\frac{3}{4}$in (18mm) to each side. Cut out. Spray the back of the paper with adhesive. Align one short edge with the base edge of the chest and smooth the paper across the base and up the side, keeping the paper straight. Continue round the chest and press the overlap to the base. Snip into the corners at the front and at each side of the drawer dividers. Smooth the overlap along the fronts of the dividers, and ease the corner and side overlaps into the chest. Neaten the corners at the back using the folded corners technique (page 102).

4 Cut strips of paper 4in (10cm) deep to fit the divider width exactly and stick across the divider edges over the overlaps and into the chest. Cut a rectangle of paper to neaten the chest back, cutting it $\frac{1}{8}$in (3mm) smaller all round than the chest measurement. Glue in place.

5 **Drawers:** Measure the inside width and depth of each drawer space and mark the shape on thin card. Measure the height of the drawer space and add to the sides of the base shape. Cut out, and score along the base lines. Fold to shape. Try out the fit of the drawer in the chest, remembering that the paper cover will add bulk. Trim if necessary. Glue the edges of drawer together and reinforce with tape. Cover the drawer using the wrap around technique, extending overlaps to become linings if desired (see page 108). Make 3 drawers.

6 **Handles:** Mark the centre of each drawer face and pierce with a sharp tool. Insert the handle fitting (or stitch a button or bead in place with strong thread). Paint gold if required. Neaten the inside front with a length of gummed tape.

7 **Drawer linings:** Measure inside drawer sides, and cut 4 strips of lining: 2 long sides with overlaps of $\frac{1}{8}$in (3mm) at each end, and all sides with $\frac{1}{8}$in (3mm) extra depth. Stick the long linings in place first, pushing well into the corners, and aligning the top edges. Add the short side linings. Measure and cut a base piece to the exact size. Press into place to stick.

PENCIL TUB
Materials
Thick card
Giftwrap paper laminated to cartridge paper
Canson (art paper) for lining
Spray adhesive, clear craft glue, gummed paper tape

1 **Tub:** Draw a $3\frac{1}{4}$in (8cm) square for the base on card. Mark $3\frac{1}{4} \times 4$in (8 × 10cm) rectangles on each side. Cut out and score along the base lines. Fold and stick the sides as for the chest.

2 Measure round the tub and cut paper to cover, $\frac{3}{8}$in (9mm) longer and 3in (7.5cm) deeper, to give an overlap of 2in (5cm) at the top and 1in (2.5cm) at the base. Spray the paper on the back. Align a $\frac{3}{8}$in (9mm) overlap round to one side and smooth the paper round until the end is level with the tub side. Cover the base corners using the folded corners technique (page 102). Cut a square for the outside base, $\frac{1}{8}$in (3mm) smaller than the base measurement.

3 **Lining:** Measure and cut linings for the tub in the same way as for lining the chest drawers and allowing $\frac{1}{8}$in (3mm) extra width on each side of two linings. Stick in place.

Tabletop stationery

Three different patterned papers are combined to make these elegant stationery designs. The details include contrast bindings and corner trims to add a practical touch in a very attractive way.

PORTFOLIO
Materials
Two co-ordinated giftwrap designs
Thick card: two rectangles 14 × 11½in (35.5 × 29.5cm)
Cartridge paper to back main paper
Thinner (copy) paper to line contrast paper.
Two sheets of Canson paper for linings in colour to blend
Grosgrain ribbon for ties, 2yds (1.80m)
Wad punch
Spray adhesive, clear craft glue, stick adhesive
½yd (50cm) of 2in (5cm)-wide self-adhesive carpet tape or
½yd (50cm) of 2–3in (5–7.5cm)-wide bookbinding or carpet tape

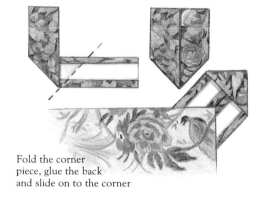

Fold the corner piece, glue the back and slide on to the corner

Position the glued flap to the back half of the portfolio, aligning the crease line ¼in (6mm) from the outside edge

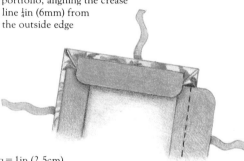

Preparation
1 Laminate the giftwrap paper to the cartridge paper with spray adhesive for the main cover. Lay the laminated paper

Graph pattern for the main flap and side flap (Scale 1 sq = 1in (2.5cm)

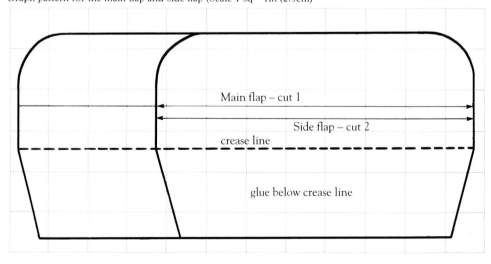

Main flap – cut 1

Side flap – cut 2

crease line

glue below crease line

flat, cartridge side facing and place the card rectangles on this, leaving at least 2in (5cm) all round, and a 1in (2.5cm) space between the cards for the spine. Pencil round the card shapes. Spray one side of each card with adhesive, and press in position on the paper

Making the portfolio

2 Peel the backing from the carpet or bookbinding tape, and place carefully over the position of the spine, overlapping each piece of card. Trim the

tape level with the card edges. Cut into the paper corners. Spread stick adhesive on the overlaps and press to the card. Ease the paper over the spine, and use your thumb nail (or a bone folder) to ease the paper into the spine creases.

3 **Protective corners:** Cut four strips 9in (23cm) long and 3$\frac{1}{4}$in (8.5cm) wide from the contrast paper. Laminate to the thin paper with spray adhesive and cut round. Mark $\frac{1}{2}$in (12mm) along each long edge and gently score and fold along the line

15

to the wrong side. Mark the centre point and fold up the sides to this point. Crease sharply so that the folded edges meet. Make 4 corner pieces in the same way. The corner pieces slot in place on the portfolio. Spread clear glue on the back triangle area of each corner, slide over and press in place on the portfolio corners. Glue the remaining overlaps and press to stick, making sure the folded edges are aligned on the wrong side.

4 Ties: With the right side of the open portfolio facing, mark the centre points on the tops and each side $\frac{3}{4}$in (2cm) from the edge. Cut through at these points with a wad punch using a $\frac{1}{4}$in (6mm) hole. Cut the ribbon into 6 equal lengths, and from the right side, thread the ribbon ends through the holes. Spread the ribbon end on the wrong side for $1\frac{1}{2}$in (4cm) and glue flat to the card with clear adhesive. Leave to dry.

5 Binding the spine: Cut a strip of cartridge paper $2\frac{1}{4}$in (6cm) by the length of the spine, plus 1in (2.5cm) on each end. Laminate to the contrast paper, allowing this to overlap by $\frac{1}{2}$in (12mm) along each side. Stick excess to the wrong side with stick adhesive, and crease the short ends in to fit the spine exactly. Spread clear glue along the wrong side of the strip and position over the spine. Press the overlaps to the wrong side, and smooth flat until secure. Alternatively, cover the spine with bookbinding or carpet tape.

6 Side flaps: Cut one long and two short flaps from the diagram. Crease the flaps gently along the glue line, and spread clear glue over the areas as marked. Position the flaps to the back half of the portfolio, placing each centrally and aligning the crease line $\frac{1}{4}$in (6mm) from the outside edge. Press flat and fold the flaps gently inwards.

7 Lining the portfolio: Measure the inside of the portfolio and cut a rectangle to reach right across the inside, leaving $\frac{1}{4}$in (6mm) all round, so that the lining is flush with the flap creases. Cut out. Stick the lining in place with spray adhesive and smooth flat, pressing the paper down into the spine fold. Open and close the portfolio several times to ease the lining into the spine. When dry, use a glue spreader to run a line of clear glue under the edges of the lining to secure it.

Finishing
8 Make a patchwork-style panel by mounting a square of contrast paper centrally on the front cover as shown in the picture. To do this, cut an 8in (20cm) square of thin paper and within this mark a $5\frac{1}{4}$in (13cm) square. Cut this centre square away to leave a frame. Stick the frame to giftwrap paper with spray adhesive, and cut round the edge leaving $\frac{1}{2}$in (12mm) extra on the outer and inner edges. Turn the excess to the wrong side, and secure with stick adhesive. Stick the frame to the portfolio with spray adhesive.

STATIONERY BOX
The instructions given are for a flip top box to hold paper and envelopes. The method is the same for any size notepaper, so you can make the box to fit your own stationery.

Materials
Thick card
Light card for the inner box
Giftwrap papers of two different designs
Cartridge paper and thin (copy) paper
Grosgrain ribbon: 5in (13cm) long and $\frac{1}{2}$in (12mm) wide
Spray adhesive, stick adhesive, tape, brown gummed paper
Notepad and envelopes

Preparation
1 Lay the notepad and envelopes side by side, and note the measurements. On light card draw a rectangle to this measurement, plus $\frac{1}{8}$in (3mm) all round. Extend $1\frac{1}{2}$in (4cm) round this for the box sides and cut out. Score along the base

lines and fold up the sides. Stick the sides together with clear adhesive and reinforce the joins with gummed paper tape.

Making the inner box

2 Laminate the first contrast paper to the cartridge paper with spray adhesive. Cover the box using the wrap around technique (see page 108), but allowing overlaps on the short sides and with the paper cut flush on the long sides. Allow sufficient top overlap to reach over to the inside base.

3 **Outer box:** Place the inner box on thick card and mark round the edges. Draw round this allowing an extra $\frac{1}{2}$in (12mm) on each short side and on one long side. Use a set square to check the right angles. Cut out, and then cut another identical rectangle. From thick card cut a strip to the same length as the rectangles, and a fraction wider than the depth of the covered inner box, to make a spine. When the spine is joined to the two rectangles they should fit easily over the inner box.

4 Place the spine strip in the centre between the two rectangles and join with gummed tape stuck on both edges along the joins. Check the flexibility – the covers should lift easily on the spine.

5 Covering the outer box: Laminate the main paper to cartridge paper. Lay the hinged card open flat on the wrong side of the giftwrap, and draw round. Mark 2in (5cm) all round the edge and cut out. Spray adhesive on the back of the giftwrap and lay the card cover over, lining up the drawn outlines. Trim the corners of the giftwrap, cutting to the corner point at a slight angle, and press the overlaps in place. Carefully ease the paper over the spine, pressing the paper well into the fold.

6 Make 4 protective corners from the first contrast paper (as for the portfolio, page 14) and stick in place. Make a protective spine in the same way, but using a paper strip to fit well over each side of box spine. Use the contrast giftwrap paper for this. Attach the spine

to the box, smoothing the overlaps into the spine crease, and flexing the cover for easy opening.

Finishing
7 Spread clear adhesive over the base of the inner box, and along one long edge for the back. Press in place inside the cover, aligning so that there is an equal overlap on each side. Twist ribbon into a loop and glue the ends under the centre lid with clear adhesive.

8 Lid lining panel: Measure the inside box, long side against the spine and the depth from the base up to within $\frac{1}{4}$in (6mm) of the lid edge. Cut a piece of cartridge paper to this size. Spray with adhesive and stick to the first contrast paper. Cut out, allowing $\frac{1}{2}$in (12mm) extra all round for turnings. Use stick adhesive to secure the turnings to the wrong side. Spray the back of the lining panel with adhesive and press the lining into place. Press well into the crease of the lid fold, and ease so that the box opens easily. Run a line of clear adhesive round the edges of the lining and press to secure.

LETTER RACK
The rack measures $9\frac{1}{2}$in (24cm) wide and $5\frac{1}{2}$in (13cm) high.

Materials
Thick card
Two sheets of giftwrap, laminated to cartridge paper
Clear craft glue, gummed brown paper tape
Self-adhesive velour or a piece of felt for the base

1 Making the rack: From card, cut a rectangle $9\frac{1}{2} \times 3$in (24×7.5cm) for the inner base. Cut the front $9\frac{1}{2} \times 2\frac{1}{4}$in ($24 \times 6$cm), the back $9\frac{1}{2} \times 5\frac{1}{2}$in ($24 \times 14$cm) and the middle divider $9\frac{1}{2} \times 3\frac{3}{4}$in ($24 \times 9.5$cm).

Draw a rectangle for the box tray base and extend the sides $1\frac{1}{2}$in (37mm). Stick the corner joins with glue and reinforce with strips

2 Run a line of glue along both long edges of the base and press the front and

Spread glue down the back and front sections
edges, press side sections in place

back sections to the glue. Reinforce the
joins with gummed tape. Leave to dry.

3 Cut the sloping side sections. Measure
the outside rack from front to back and
mark this on card. Draw a line from the
height of the front edge to the height of
the back edge. Cut out. Cut another
section to match. Run a line of glue
down the edges of the back and front
sections, and along the edges of the base.
Press side sections in place. Reinforce
with gummed tape.

4 Lining the rack: Start by covering the
inside sloping sides. Draw round the side
shapes on cartridge side of paper and cut
out (making sure you have a left and a
right side) $\frac{3}{4}$in (18mm) longer at the top
and base, and $\frac{1}{8}$in (3mm) wider on each
side. Spray paper with adhesive and press
into position, pushing the paper well into
corners. Pleat and press paper over to the
outside at the top corners. Do not cut –
smooth flat.

5 Cut paper to line the inside back. Cut
to exact inside width with $\frac{1}{4}$in (6mm)
extra base and $\frac{3}{4}$in (18mm) overlap at the
top. Spray with adhesive and press into
position.

6 Cut paper to line the inside front
allowing $\frac{1}{4}$in (6mm) overlap at the base,
$\frac{3}{4}$in (18mm) overlap at the front and with

the side measurements to fit exactly.
Stick in place. Cut a rectangle to fit inside
the base exactly. Stick in place.

7 Covering the outside: Measure round
the outside rack from the front edge
round to the other front edge. Draw the
shape on to the back of paper. Add $\frac{1}{2}$in
(12mm) overlaps on all sides, and crease
inwards along the top drawn line. Stick
the turnings flat with stick adhesive,
snipping into corners as necessary. Coat
the back of the paper with spray
adhesive. Place the front edge overlap to
the front of the rack, and smooth the
paper round to the other side. Snip the
base overlap to the corners, angle cut and
then press to the base.

8 Measure across the front and cut paper
to the exact size plus $\frac{1}{2}$in (12mm) overlap
at the top edge and base. Spray with
adhesive and press into position. Snip the
front corner to reach over to the inside.

9 Divider: Cut paper to twice the depth
of the card, and $\frac{1}{2}$in (12mm) wider on
each side. Cut out. Spray the back with
adhesive and wrap round the card. Press
flat, pressing the side overlaps together.
Crease these at right angles to divider.
Trim the top edges of the flaps to a slight
angle.

10 Pencil a mark midway between the
front and back on the inside rack side.
Draw a vertical line at this point. Spread
adhesive on the outer edge of each
divider flap and align with the vertical
lines. Press to stick.

11 Plinth: Measure and cut a card
rectangle, $\frac{1}{4}$in (6mm) larger all round than
the rack base. Cover with paper using the
folded corner method (page 103) and
turning the overlaps to the wrong side of
the base. Neaten the underside with a
piece of self-adhesive velour or felt.
Spread glue evenly over the rack base and
position centrally on the plinth. Press
until dry.

TWO

Home Decor

❦

Shady looks

Concertina pleats are simple to make, and ideal for shaping into lampshades, as their understated looks blend easily with most decorating styles. This shade uses a patterned giftwrap paper.

The instructions are for a lampshade frame measuring 16in (40cm) at base, and 4in (10cm) at top, and about 8in (20cm) high. The paper shade which fits over is made deeper than this. The method of construction is the same whatever the frame size – follow these instructions and simply increase or decrease the length and depth of pleated paper to fit round your particular frame.

Materials
Four sheets A2 cartridge paper
Four sheets of giftwrap paper
1¼yd (1m) narrow toning or contrasting
   cord or ribbon
Stationery single-hole punch
Stick adhesive
Spray adhesive

Preparation
1 Spray one side of a cartridge sheet with adhesive, and carefully lay a sheet of giftwrap over. Smooth flat. Repeat with other three sheets, aligning the design motifs on each one. When dry trim papers to 14in (36cm) deep.

2 On the back of the cartridge paper, measure and draw out pleats as 1in (2.5cm) divisions across width (see page 104). Trim the short edge of the paper to the size of the pleat if necessary. Repeat with the other sheets.

3 **Making the shade:** On the back of each sheet mark a line across the width 1in (2.5cm) from one long edge of the paper to mark the gathering line. Score pleats lightly along the drawn lines. Fold up into crisp concertina pleats. Join each sheet together with stick adhesive,

overlapping the end pleats to make a long strip.

4 Turn the joined strip to the wrong side, and use a hole punch to punch holes through the folded pleats, reaching as close to the centre of each pleat as possible. When complete use the punch

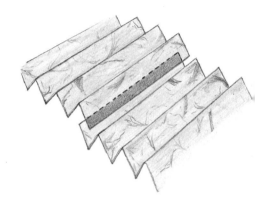

Overlap and glue the last pleat under the new paper edge to extend the length. Continue pleating

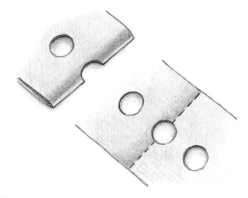

After punching holes through the middle of pleats, punch half a hole on the pleat fold

to punch half a hole at the edge of each pleat fold, in between the other holes. These edge holes will fit on to the frame top.

5 Run cord or ribbon through the holes, and check the fit of the shade round the frame. Extra pleated lengths of paper can be added at this stage if the pleats are not 'sitting well', or do not reach evenly round the frame. If the fit is good, release the cord and glue the remaining pleat ends together. Adjust the punched holes

if necessary on the last joined pleats, and re-thread the cord. Tie in a double knot to secure when the shade is sitting well on the frame. Push the knots to the wrong side, or tie the ends in a decorative bow.

Frame it

The relief textures on this papier mâché picture frame are achieved with cords, paper balls and tissue paper.

Materials

Strong cardboard for frame base 10 × 8in (25.5 × 20.5cm)
Newsprint torn into strips, 4 × 1in (10 × 2.5cm)
Prepared paste with added PVA
50 compressed paper balls, ½in (12mm) diameter
One sheet of good quality tissue paper larger than frame
Thick piping cord
Emulsion paint; enamel paints in one main shade and three other colours for sponging; clear varnish
Small pieces of sponge
Card for frame backing and strut
Artist's cover paper in shade to match the frame
Sheet of acetate for the window
PVA and clear craft glue

Making the frame

1 Cut a 6½ × 4½in (16.5 × 11.5cm) window aperture in the centre of the card frame. Spread both sides of newspaper strips with paste and wrap round the card frame, building up layers on the right side and keeping the back flat. After adding 3 layers leave to dry, then continue adding layers until the frame front has a slight curve. Leave to dry after every three layers. Neaten and smooth the frame back by applying strips to build the shape flat and level, with strip overlaps at the sides. Leave to dry.

2 **Adding moulding:** Run a line of PVA around the edge of the window aperture and press a length of piping cord to this. Make a join at one corner, and neaten the cut ends with PVA. Check the cord is lying straight, with matching curves at the corners. Add cord to the outside edge in the same way. When dry, cover the cords with long strips of paste-soaked newsprint, smoothing the ends to the wrong side of the frame. Leave to dry.

3 Add balls. Use PVA to secure one at each corner between the cords, and stick other balls in between, gluing them to the frame and to each other where they touch. Check alignment and leave to dry.

4 Paint a thin layer of paste over the frame, and on to one side of the tissue paper. Carefully lay the tissue paper, paste side down, over the frame. Gently tear away the tissue from the window area. Using fingers and gentle pressure, ease the tissue smoothly over the balls and into the spaces between. Press tissue round and over the frame surface, trimming and tucking the excess to the wrong side. Leave to dry.

5 **Painting the frame:** Paint emulsion on the right side of the frame. Leave to dry, then paint the wrong side. Paint the right side of the frame with 2 coats of base colour enamel paint and leave to dry.

6 Pour a little of the first sponging colour on to a small plate. Sponge colour all over the right side of the frame. Colour will adhere readily to raised areas.

Draw the strut from this pattern.

Scale: 1 square = 1 sq inch (2.5cm)

Frame strut
Cut 1 from card
fold

Leave to dry. Apply a second and third colour in the same way, emphasizing selected areas with extra colour. Paint the back of the frame with base colour and leave to dry.

7 Frame backing: Cut a rectangle from card to fit the back of the frame. Cut cover paper to cover this, allowing an extra ½in (12mm) for turnings all round. Fix to the card with spray adhesive and glue the turnings, using the folded corner method (page 103).

8 Make a strut so that the frame can be used vertically or horizontally. Cut card using the pattern given as a guide. Score a fold line 1in (2.5cm) from the straight end to make a hinge. Cover the scored

side with paper as before, smoothing it into the fold line and pressing the overlaps to wrong side. Cut the lining, to the same width as the strut, and the length to just above the score line. Glue in place. Place the strut on the frame back and lightly mark the position. Glue the back of the hinge and press to the backing to stick.

Finishing
9 Cut acetate slightly larger than the window aperture. Stick to the back of the frame with a little adhesive round the edges. Leave to dry.

10 Join the backing to the frame with a little adhesive run round 3 sides, leaving one side unglued to insert the picture.

Border lines

These pretty paper friezes can be used to edge shelves, pressed flat for border trims on walls – or divided into single motifs to decorate greetings cards.

Materials
Lightweight paper (copy or typing paper
  or good quality tissue paper)
Scissors with small, pointed blades
Scalpel
Stapler

Preparation
1 Trace the required pattern on to one end of a sheet of paper, so that the pattern fold is level with the short edge. Mark all the areas to be cut out. Crease the paper into concertina folds making sure the edges are at right angles. Secure the layers by stapling them together above and below the pattern area.

Cutting out
2 Using a scalpel, cut out the smallest areas inside the pattern first. For accurate, sharply defined shapes, cut from each corner of the marked shape. Make sure the scalpel blade pierces through all layers. Cut out other small shapes with scissors. Cut out the design outlines last. Discard the excess paper and stapled areas.

Finishing
3 Continue steps 1 and 2 until you have required length of motifs. To join strips, either overlap the motifs to match and secure with a little adhesive at the back, or trim the motifs as necessary, and butt-join the edges. Secure along the back with sticky tape.

4 You can iron the finished length of frieze and mount it on to a contrasting colour paper. Cut above and below the frieze, leaving a narrow band of contrast colour to accentuate the pattern.

Trace the design against the short edge, concertina-fold the paper and staple

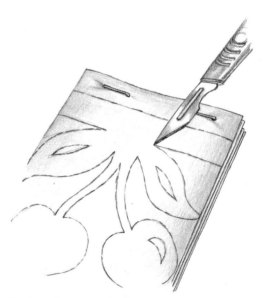

Cut from the corner of a shape using a scalpel blade

Trace these full-sized shapes for the friezes

Vista

fold

fold

Cherries

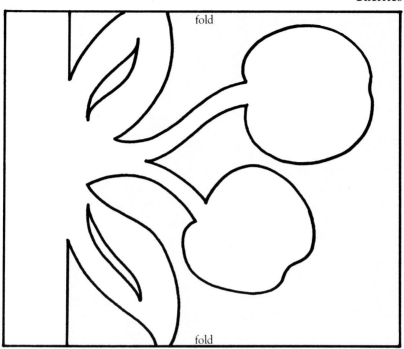

fold

fold

Leaves

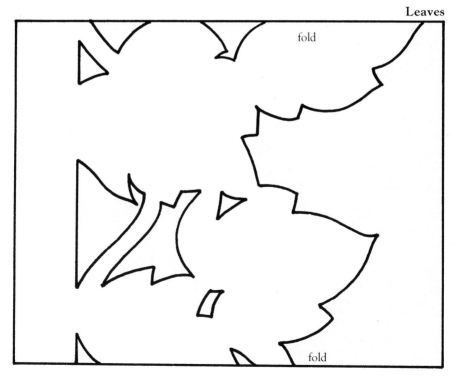

fold

fold

29

All tied up

Paper ribbon comes into its own as smart laced trims on these pretty print containers. Make them in two sizes as a matching pair, and use them to hold a host of clutter in a decorative way!

Materials
For both containers:
Artist's mounting card (or other thick card)
Large hole wad punch, hammer and board
Spray adhesive, spray fixative (optional)
For large container:
Two sheets of giftwrap
6yds (5.5m) paper ribbon
For small container:
One sheet of giftwrap
3¾yds (3.5m) paper ribbon

Preparation
1 On card, mark out the base shape 4½in (11cm) square and extend the lines as shown in the diagram. Cut out round the outside shape, and score along the fold lines. Fold up to shape.

Making the containers
2 To cover the container sides, lay the card flat, scored side down, on the wrong side of the giftwrap. Draw round one side, down to the base crease. Remove the card. Measure a line 1½in (4cm) round the drawn outline, and cut out. Cut 3 more shapes the same and set aside. Spray the wrong side of the paper with adhesive and lay the paper sticky side up on the work surface. Press the card shape on to the paper, aligning the drawn outline.

3 Carefully snip the overlaps at an angle at the base crease as shown, and fold the side overlaps to inside. Ease the base overlap gently over the crease line and stick to the base. Use the folded corner method (page 103) to neaten the overlaps on the top edge. Repeat the procedure to cover the other three sides.

4 Measure and cut a square of giftwrap to cover the outside of the base. It should fit exactly. Stick in place.

5 **Linings:** To make the inside linings, measure from just below the top inside edge to the base crease, then add 1in (2.5cm) for the inside base overlap. Make the lining width the same as the side

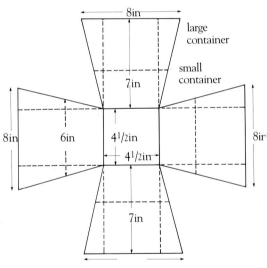

Ease the base overlap gently over the crease line, stick down

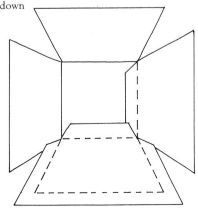

measurement. Cut out 4 linings to these measurements from giftwrap. Trim the edges slightly on each side so that they fit the container without going right to the card edges. Spray with adhesive on the wrong side and fit in place. Ease into the crease line at the base. Trim the corners of the base overlaps as you stick them in place, to reduce bulk. Cut a square of giftwrap to line inside the base, spray and stick in position.

Finishing

6 Large container: On one side edge, mark a dot for a hole close to the base crease, and another near the top edge. Position dots $\frac{1}{2}$in (12mm) in from the side edge. Measure and mark 5 more equally spaced dots between. Mark the same positions on both edges of each side piece.

7 Small container: Mark a dot near the base and at the top of the sides, as for the large container, and position one dot in between.

8 Both containers: Resting each container side over a protective surface (a chopping board or a piece of wood), use a wad punch to punch holes at the dot positions.

9 Do not unfurl the ribbon yet. Divide and cut the ribbon into 4 equal lengths. To lace two side pieces together, thread the ribbon through opposite holes at the base, and lace up to the top. At the top edges, unfurl the ribbon ends. Lace all four sides in the same way and tie in generous bows, resting the bow knot on the top edge of the container. Trim bow ends as desired.

Crazy tray

Give an old tray a fresh look or personalize a new one. Crazy patchwork and the textiles of the 1920s inspired this découpage design cut from giftwrap and coloured foils.

Materials

A wood or metal tray
Selection of giftwrap papers and coloured
  foils protected with spray fixative
Wallpaper paste mixed full strength
Fine sandpaper, finest gauge wire wool
Clear household varnish
Wax polish

Preparation

1 If you are revamping an old tray, sand down any flaky surfaces, and repaint the edges and base using an appropriate paint.

2 Take a tracing of the base shape as a pattern when cutting out the design pieces.

Working the design

3 Use a craft knife or scissors to cut a selection of larger shapes from giftwrap, sufficient to cover the base of the tray. Overlap or butt-join the edges, but avoid overlaps of more than two layers. Be careful when placing light colours over darker patterns as they may show through. The design is worked at random as the term 'crazy' suggests, but it is a good idea to turn the tray round as you work, to vary the direction of the design.

4 Paste the back of the large paper pieces, and arrange them on the tray. Smooth away any air bubbles, and continue adding shapes and smoothing the surface as you work. Cut out foil shapes using a craft knife and straight edge, and arrange these over the giftwrap. Continue adding shapes until you feel the design is complete.

5 Place a sheet of plain paper over the design, and press the design all over to remove any remaining air bubbles, using firm pressure with the palm of the hand. Leave work to dry completely.

Finishing

6 Apply a thin coat of varnish over the design and leave to dry in an airy place away from dust. Apply another coat of varnish, and when dry, gently rub over the surface with sandpaper. Wipe clean, and repeat with another two coats of varnish. Continue in this way, varnishing and lightly sanding until the varnish creates a smooth and perfectly even layer over the paper shapes. Ten or twelve coats of varnish should give the required effect. Finish the tray by rubbing lightly with wire wool. Finish with wax polish to shine.

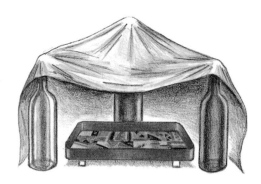

Make a 'tent' of plastic sheeting to protect the piece from dust

Evergreen garland

Soft woodland colours are touched with gold to create a winter garland. The understated subtle glints add a celebratory air, so the design would make an attractive Christmas decoration.

Materials
Twisted vine wreath, 10in (25cm)
   diameter
Gold paint (brush-on or spray)
Gold felt tip marker pen
White double crêpe paper
Soft, dark green paper ribbon
Green flowermaking tape
Flower stem wires
Spool of binding wire
White pearlized flower stamens
Stick adhesive, UHU glue, PVA glue
Glitter dust
Cord to hang wreath

Preparation
1 Paint the wreath gold and leave to dry. Apply glitter by painting vine stems with PVA. Sprinkle glitter on to the glue and leave to dry. Tie a small cord loop to the back to hang the wreath.

Making the garland
2 Leaves: Trace the leaf patterns and draw on to thin card and cut out for templates. Cut 10 stem wires in half. Bind each piece with green tape. For the largest size leaf cut a 2½in (6cm) length of unravelled paper ribbon and spread stick adhesive on one half. Lay the bound wire on the glue centrally. Fold the paper ribbon over and press flat with hand. Fold the leaf in half along the stem. Using the largest leaf template cut round through both layers. Open the leaf flat. Colour the leaf on the surface with a gold marker pen. Make 6 large leaves, 8 medium-sized leaves and 6 small leaves in the same way. You will require a shorter length of ribbon for the smaller leaves.

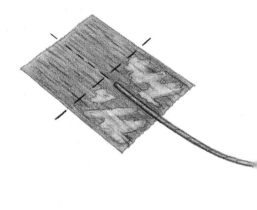

Fold the paper ribbon over the stem wire, fold along the wire and cut out the ivy leaves

LARGE FLOWER
Cut 3 from white double crepe paper

SMALL FLOWER
Cut 3 from white double crepe paper

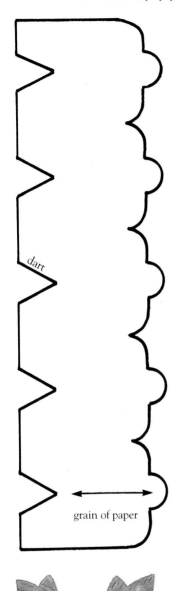

dart

grain of paper

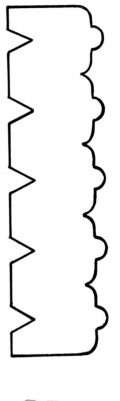

Stroke gold marker pen from the petals base to the centre. Glue the darts together to shape the flower

Twist 3 small leaves together, then twist in a medium-sized leaf

36

3 The garland is decorated with 2 sprays of leaves, each spray having 10 leaves in a mixture of the three sizes. To join the leaves into a spray, take 3 small leaves and twist the stems together. Wire-in a medium-sized leaf, then another in the same way, so that the stem gradually lengthens. Continue joining-in new leaves on each side of the stem, finishing with the largest leaves. Arrange the spray into a natural position, and set aside. Make another spray in the same way.

4 Flowers: Trace the flower patterns and make templates from thin card. Cut 3 large and 3 small petal sections from white crêpe paper. Bind a half length of stem wire with green tape. Fold 6 stamens (3 for smaller flowers) in half and bend the stem end over them to secure. Mould each petal shape by gently stretching each one sideways between thumbs. Stroke gold marker pen from base to centre on each petal. When the ink is dry, spread clear adhesive along the lower petal edge, and bring the dart edges together to shape the flower. Gather up the glued flower around the prepared stem and stamens, and press to stick. Wrap green tape round the base of the petals to secure them to the stem, and to suggest a calyx. Make the other flowers in the same way.

Finishing
5 Arrange the ivy leaves on each side of the wreath and attach the sprays with short lengths of binding wire, placed inconspicuously behind the leaves. Wire in the flowers in the same way, arranging them to mingle with the ivy leaves.

IVY LEAVES
Cut from green paper ribbon

Keep blades keen by sharpening them on a sharpening block. The blade is held at an angle and gently drawn across the surface. Sharpen first one side of the blade then turn the knife over and sharpen the other. Wipe blades with a little machine oil when they are not in use. Clean them off with a rag before a project.

Baskets for fun

Paper can be woven or plaited to make decorative – and useful – baskets. Both designs can be scaled up or down in size.

WOVEN BASKET

Materials

Canson paper, or similar weight of art paper in 5 different colours, cut into 14 strips 24in (61cm) × 1in (2.5cm) (Cut at least two strips from each colour)
Magazine colour pages, laminated to cartridge paper
Metallic cords and threads
Clear craft glue
Paper clips

Preparation

1 In weaving, the woven strips which run vertically are called the warp, and those which run from right to left across these are called the weft. Lay 5 warp strips of art papers side by side, ends level, in your chosen colour sequence. Weave 5 more art paper strips over and under these, following the colour sequence. Push the strips tightly together, checking that the corners are at right angles. Fold the strips inwards around the edges to mark the base edge.

Making the basket

2 To weave the basket sides, hold the side strips vertically and weave a new strip through. Crease the strip at each corner to help to hold the square shape. Push the strips down to the base and overlap the ends behind a vertical strip. Trim and secure the overlaps together with glue. Hold them with paper clips until the glue is dry. Repeat with the other three strips.

3 **Contrast strips:** Cut the laminated magazine pages into narrow strips, some ¾in (18mm) wide and others ½in (12mm) wide. Cut some plainer colour strips to the same sizes, and some ¼in (6mm) wide.

4 Weave the contrast strips as desired through basket weave. Secure the ends of the strips woven round the basket sides by overlapping and gluing as before. Secure the vertical ends by gluing them to the basket weave just above the top edge. Weave gold threads on top, or

Weave the sides, creasing at the corners. Overlap and glue the ends behind a vertical strip

For the diamond edge, fold the vertical strip, crease and then weave into the basket side

beside contrast strips. Glue the vertical thread ends to the top edge, and knot the ends of threads worked round basket. Push the knots out of sight behind the weave.

5 Diamond edging: With the outside of the basket facing, and working from left to right, start work on the first strip in from a corner. Fold a warp strip over towards you so that the strip edge is level with the edge of the top warp strip. Crease the fold, and fold the strip back to the inside of the basket to shape a triangle. Crease to shape. Weave the ends into the weave inside basket, and trim away the excess neatly. Work round the basket in this way, creasing the centre of each corner triangle to shape.

6 Basket handle: Cut three 22in (56cm) strips of different coloured art papers to match the basket: one ¾in (18mm) wide and two 1in (2.5cm) wide. Lay the strips one on another, and secure the layers at each end with clear glue. Lay pieces of metallic thread along the length and glue down at the ends. Wrap small lengths of contrast coloured strip across the handle in the middle and half way between the middle and the ends. Glue the strips together on the underside of the handle. Tuck one end of the handle into the side of the basket on the outside, positioning it behind the centre weave on the second-from-top horizontal weave. Pull the end of the handle through the weave and check that the handle middle is centred. Adjust the handle to the required height. Tuck the end over into the top of the weave and trim excess as necessary. Repeat on other side of the handle.

BRAIDED BASKET

Materials

Three coils of 2in (5cm)-wide paper
   ribbon in three different shades
Thin, sharp sewing needle; thimble or
   leather glove
Rubber bands
Clear craft glue

Preparation

1 Unfurl the paper ribbons. Hold the
ends of 3 lengths of ribbon together (one
of each colour) with rubber bands. Plait
the ribbons together keeping the tension
even so that the ribbon stays plumped
and pliable.

Making the basket

2 To start coiling, remove the rubber
band from the end of the braid and glue
the ends tightly together, keeping the
plait formation. When quite dry, cut
away the excess to leave a small neat
stump. This will be the centre base of the
basket.

3 Working on a flat surface, begin
coiling the braid into shape. Thread a
needle with a double thread and anchor
the end under the plait stump with a
back stitch. Wear a thimble (or leather
glove) for the next stage: keeping the
braid flat, work the needle back and forth
between the sides of the braid pulling the
thread quite tightly between the stitches
to bring the braid sides together so that
the thread does not show. Work 4 or 5
rounds for the basket base.

4 To build the basket sides position the
braid at a slight angle to the edge of the
last base braid, and stitch to hold
position. Continue stitching round in the
same way as before to the desired depth.
Finish stitching within 6in (15cm) of your
chosen finishing point.

5 Trim the braid ends and secure with a
rubber band. Pinch the ribbon ends
together and secure with glue (as you did
at stage 2). Trim the ends neatly.
Continue stitching to the end of the

braid, gradually working-in the tapered
end stump. Work the thread ends back
into the braid so that they do not show.

Handles

6 Position these to help disguise the
finishing point. Make handles by plaiting
braids in the same 3 colours as the
basket, or plait one-colour braids as a
contrast. Secure the ends as before, and
plait the handle to the required length.
(Braids should be long enough to form a
deep loop without stretching or pulling).
Finish off the ends as before, and secure
with glue. Make 2 handles. Bend the
handles and sew to the inside of the
basket on opposite sides. Use matching
doubled sewing thread.

Add ribbon strips by opening the end
flat, open the end of new piece, overlap
ends and glue together

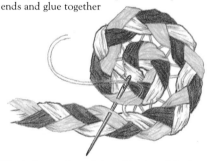

Work the needle and thread back and forth
between the sides of the braid

Joining-in lengths

To join-in a length, flatten out and
then overlap the ribbon ends. Secure
with adhesive. Extra lengths can be
added and plaited at any stage in this
way, even when the basket is being
stitched to shape. Stagger the colour
sequence so that joins occur in
different places.

Paper roses

Spoil yourself, or someone you love, with a bouquet of gorgeous paper blooms, or make a single rose as an impressive trim on a very special gift. Choose harmonious natural colours for a realistic look, or make fantasy roses in gold and silver for festive occasions.

Materials

Double crêpe paper, in two-tone shades (red/crimson, coral/light coral, deep pink/light pink)
Art paper, such as cover paper, in leaf green
Clear glue
Flower stem wire
Spool of binding wire
Green flowermaking tape
Cotton wool

Preparation

1 Holding the tape diagonally to a stem wire, wrap the tape down the stem. Bend one end of the wire into a hook. Wrap with a little cotton wool to make bud shape, then cover with a square of crêpe paper in your chosen colour. Secure the edges of the paper down the stem with binding wire.

Making the rose

2 Trace the petal shape and cut from thin card for a template. Use the template to cut out 12 petals. With the darkest shade of the crêpe paper facing away from you, shape each petal by gently stretching it sideways between your thumbs, to cup the petal shape. Then carefully stroke the petal over a scissor blade to curve the top edge outwards.

3 Spread glue round the inside base of one petal and wrap it tightly round the centre 'bud' and stem. Attach each petal by spreading glue across the base, and arrange them opposite one another, and overlapping until all twelve are in place.

4 Bind the bases of the petals tightly in place with binding wire, wrapping the

wire down round the stem for a short way. Wrap green tape over the wire and down the stem to cover the binding wire.

5 Sepals: Trace the sepal shape and cut 5 sepals from green paper. Stretch and curl the sepals over a scissor blade. Spread glue on the broad end of each sepal and wrap each one round the top of the stem, arranging them evenly, and pressing them to stick. Secure by wrapping green tape round the base of the sepals, and continue taping down the stem to end, then back up again to top edge of tape, to thicken the stem.

6 Leaves: Trace the leaf shapes and cut from thin card for templates. Use the templates to cut from double thickness green paper. Use the templates to cut one large and two small leaves. Cut a stem wire in half, and bend one piece in the middle to a 'v'. Place the bent piece over the stem half as shown. Bind the stems with green tape to hold position.

7 Spread glue over one large leaf shape and press it to the centre wire. Spread glue on a second large leaf shape and press over the first leaf, enclosing the wire. When dry, use small sharp scissors to make small cuts around the edge of the leaf to suggest a serrated outline. Repeat the process with the smaller leaves, Attach the leaf stem to the rose stem with green tape. Bend the flower and leaf stems to shape them realistically.

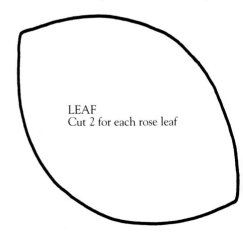

LEAF
Cut 2 for each rose leaf

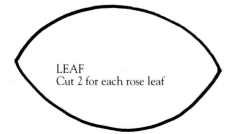

LEAF
Cut 2 for each rose leaf

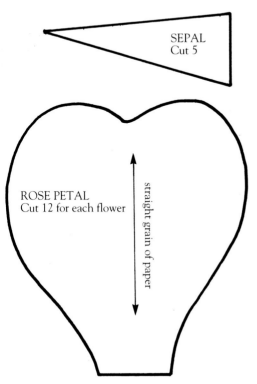

SEPAL
Cut 5

ROSE PETAL
Cut 12 for each flower

straight grain of paper

Cover the hook with cotton wool then crêpe paper. Wire to secure

Stretch each petal sideways between the thumbs to cup the shape

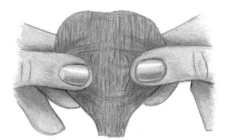

43

Fruit bowl

Unusual bowls can be moulded with wallpaper, and decorated inside and out with tissue, sparkle-textured Japanese paper and gems. Make an arrangement of fruit from papier mâché also and perhaps play a joke on your friends.

BOWL
Materials
Deep bowl with flat base for mould
Wall lining paper
PVA adhesive
Japanese paper: white with gold and
   silver flecks, purple textured
Navy blue art paper
Yellow tissue paper
Flat backed gems: black, topaz and
   diamonds

Preparation
1 Prepare the mould and tear the wallpaper into strips. Dilute the PVA to a creamy consistency with water. Work 8 layers of papier mâché over the mould. When completely dry remove the work from the mould and trim the edges level.

2 Neaten the edge of the bowl by pasting strips of lining paper over it to soften the effect. Leave to dry.

3 **Decorating the bowl:** Tear strips and patches from Japanese and other papers and arrange and paste these as desired around the inside of the bowl. Make use of colour changes and effects created by overlapping a light colour such as yellow on purple and navy. Try tearing away some of the nearly dry paper to reveal colour stains created on the underlying paper. Take some paper shapes over the top edge of the bowl so the design appears to flow over to the outside surface. When you are satisfied with the effect, brush over the surface with a coat of diluted PVA. Leave to dry thoroughly.

4 Decorate the outside bowl in the same way. Balance the bowl on a prop, and paste shapes in place. Brush over with diluted PVA solution and leave to dry.

5 Make a stiffer solution of PVA and use this to attach gems round the outside of the bowl (avoiding the base). When dry, repeat the process inside the bowl. Brush over all surfaces with two more coats of PVA and allow to dry thoroughly.

FUN FRUIT
Materials
Any firm fruit: apples, pears, bunch of
   bananas
Newspaper strips, paste with added PVA
Petroleum jelly (vaseline)
Craft knife and kitchen knife
PVA, masking tape and fine sandpaper
Water based paints: emulsion paint,
   acrylic, watercolours or poster paints,
Watercolour brushes, optional stencil
   brush
Varnish

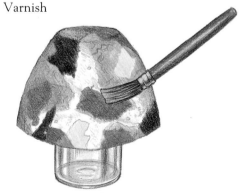

Prop the upturned bowl on a jar, paste the coloured paper shapes on the surface

Preparation

1 Coat the piece of fruit with petroleum jelly. Dampen the paper strips with water, then apply to the fruit. Work round the stalk pressing the paper strips well into the contours of the fruit.

Working the design

2 Build up 3 layers of paper strips using paste, then leave to dry naturally on a wire rack. (Do not dry in oven or near direct heat, as this could cause the fruit to disintegrate.) Add 3 more layers of paper strips. Allow to dry then add 2 more layers, making 8 layers altogether. Leave to dry completely.

45

3 Starting at the stalk of the fruit, use a craft knife to slit the papier mâché, working from stalk to base and back up to the stalk. Insert the tip of a kitchen knife into the slit and cut through the fruit. Gently prise the fruit from each half, and clear the inside of the mould of any fruit remains. Mark each mould half with a symbol of easy matching. Repeat with the other fruit.

4 Run a line of PVA round one cut edge of the fruit shape and press to other half to join. Secure with small strips of masking tape until dry. When dry, remove the tape and reinforce the join by covering it with strips of PVA-coated paper. Use more strips to cover the stalk points on the fruit, smoothing them to blend with the surface. Leave to dry. Check over the surface for any rough patches, and smooth with sandpaper if necessary.

Painting fruit
5 Prepare the fruit with a light base coat of water-based paint ready for decoration. You can try your hand at adding a colourful blush to the fruit, but if you are not entirely happy with your artistic skills, opt for plain colours – green or red apples, and bright yellow bananas – they will still look good!

6 Bananas: Paint in a basic shade of yellow. When dry, work the dark ends and greenish shading along the sides. Smudge the colours with your fingers and use a dampened brush to blend the colours naturally. Dab-on small brown 'ripe' spots at random. To re-assemble a bunch, select a few bananas which fit together well, and join them at the sides of each stalk with PVA. Hold in position until dry with masking tape. Soak a small piece of paper with PVA, and crumple it. Stick this across the stalk ends. When dry, paint it brown to match the stalks. Varnish fruit when the paint is dry.

7 Apples: Pierce a small hole in the top of the fruit. Make a stalk by tightly rolling a small strip of PVA-soaked paper. Leave to dry. Coat one end of the stalk with PVA and push into the top of the fruit. Paint the apple an all-over shade of green or red, then work flecks and smudged stripes of shaded green or red down over the fruit. Paint the stalk and the old sepals at the base of the fruit in a brown shade. Varnish when dry.

8 Pears: Make stalks in the same way as for apples. Paint the pear an all-over shade of golden green, and smudge on touches of red or green with your fingers. Alternatively, use an almost dry stencil brush to add colour and texture. Varnish when dry.

Starting at the stalk end, slit the papier mâché shell all round using a crafts knife

Glue the two half apples together, then paste strips over the join

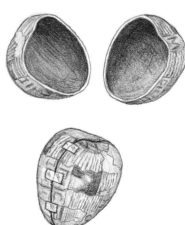

Chintz prints

These découpage candlesticks and the matching ornament are decorated with flowers cut from an antique, chintz-patterned giftwrap. The flowers were chosen for their subtle colouring, and arranged to follow and flatter the underlying shapes.

Materials

Wooden or ceramic candlesticks, ceramic
  ornament
Giftwrap paper protected with spray
  fixative
Small pair of curved manicure scissors
Pair of tweezers
Wallpaper paste mixed to full strength
Multi-purpose gold paint
Finest gauge wire wool, fine sandpaper
Clear, satin-finish varnish

Preparation

1 Cut out a selection of motifs, bearing
in mind the curves and shapes of the
candlestick and ornament which the
paper cut-outs must cover without
pleating or distorting. Choose small
motifs, and overlap them to make a
larger design area as required. Handle
very small shapes with tweezers.

2 Gently rub down wooden surfaces
with sandpaper, and wipe clean. Ceramic
surfaces should be washed to remove
surface grease, and thoroughly dried.
Paint ceramic surfaces with gold paint,
and leave to dry.

Working the design

3 Use the shape of the objects to suggest
the placing of the paper cut-outs. These
candlesticks have wide bases and
moulding on the stems, giving the
opportunity to decorate these parts with
plenty of pattern. The ceramic duck has a
broad, curved back, so a garland of small
flowers is built up to emphasize this
shape, while the eye detail lends a
realistic touch to the more fanciful
design.

4 Paste larger motifs to the candlesticks,
arranging duplicate shapes so they
balance evenly in the design. When
decorating a pair of candlesticks, work
on both at the same time to ensure an
even distribution of shapes. As you paste
shapes in place, smooth the surface to
release any air bubbles. Gradually add
the design, turning the object round
periodically to check that the design is

well balanced. When complete, leave to
dry.

Finishing

5 Paint the object with a thin coat of
varnish and leave to dry away from dust
and direct heat. Varnish awkward shapes
which need turning over (like the duck) a
little at a time, allowing parts to dry
before continuing. Repeat with another 2
coats and leave to dry. When dry, rub
very carefully and lightly with sand paper
to give a surface key, and then continue
with 3 more thin layers of varnish.
Repeat sanding and varnishing until the
cut edges of the motifs can no longer be
felt with a finger. Twelve to fourteen
coats of varnish should be sufficient.
Finish the pieces by rubbing lightly with
wire wool, and then polish to a shine
with wax polish.

Cut out tiny motifs using nail scissors with curved
blades

Découpage can also be worked on
the reverse side of clear glass items.
Paper cut-outs are pasted to the
inside of glass containers or the
backs of glass panels or plates. When
the paste is dry, dab matt paint in a
neutral colour – cream, beige or pale
grey-green – all over the cut-out and
glass. Plates look as though they had
been hand-painted with motifs and
glass containers look like decorated
porcelain.

49

THREE

Jewellery

Paper beads

These beads are made from long strips of rolled paper. You can use almost any weight of paper, in patterns or plains. The strips can be rolled singly, as here, or together in pairs to create two-tone effects. The metallic giftwrap used to shape these beads makes them look like shiny enamel.

Materials
Sheet of good quality plastic foil giftwrap
Knitting needle (the diameter smaller
    than the metal bead size)
Petroleum jelly
Thirty $\frac{1}{4}$in (5mm)-diameter gold metal
    beads
Necklace fastening
Bead stringing thread
Beading needle
Stick adhesive

Make two extra beads for earrings.
Make them the same size or from
wide paper strips as a contrast.
Thread a metal bead on to a jewellery
wire with a hook or eye end, and
pass the wire through the paper bead.
Thread on another metal bead and
attach wire to earring fitting.

Preparation
1 From giftwrap, cut 15 strips to the
dimensions shown using a ruler and
sharp craft knife. Taper the strips equally
on each side. This ensures the bead will
shape evenly when it is rolled.

2 Smear petroleum jelly on the knitting
needle. Stroke adhesive along the entire
wrong side of the paper strip. Starting at
the widest end, roll the strip tightly
round the needle. Make sure it is rolling
evenly, and adjust if necessary. Secure
the end with a little more adhesive.
Gently slide the bead off the needle.

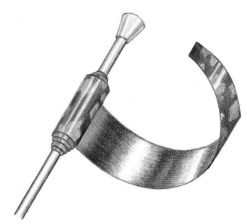

Roll the glued strip of gift paper round a knitting
needle

3 Make 15 beads in the same way.
Arrange them in a line, and place any
beads which may look larger in the centre
of the line.

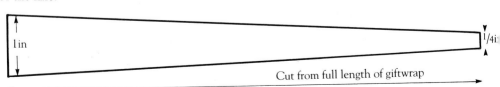

1in

$^{1}/_{4}$in

Cut from full length of giftwrap

Stringing the beads

4 Thread a beading needle with a long length of bead thread. Thread 1 metal bead, 1 paper bead, 2 metal, 1 paper, 2 metal, until the last single metal bead. Knot the thread to one half of the necklace fastening. Thread the end back down into the beads for 3in (7.5cm) and trim the end. Slide beads along the thread so that they are as close as possible. Pass the end of the thread through the other half of fastening. Knot then thread the end back into the beads for 3in (7.5cm). Trim the end.

All that glitters

Make an impressive set of fashion accessories with papier mâché, metallic paints, beads and clever touches with a gold colour marker.

Materials
Card tube 3¼in (8.5cm) diameter cut to
   1in (2.5cm) deep
Thin card, corrugated card
Decorative upholstery nails
Paper balls 1¼in (3cm) diameter
Eighteen compressed paper balls ½in
   (12mm) diameter
Dark grey metallic paint; black enamel
   paint
Large tipped gold marker
Clear varnish, emulsion paint
Superglue
Jewellery findings: necklace thread and
   catch, brooch pin or hair clip
Twenty small gold beads for necklace
Prepared paste mixed with PVA
Glitter fabric decorating pen

1 Pewter and gold bangle: Paste newspaper strips round the card tube. Build up extra layers on the outside to curve the shape. Leave to dry.

2 Paint the bangle with undercoat. Leave to dry. Paint the entire bangle with metallic grey paint.

3 Follow the picture to draw curved shapes round bangle with the gold marker pen. Colour-in the drawn outlines and run gold along one edge. Leave to dry. Mark gold spots over remaining grey area and colour along the other edge. Leave to dry.

4 Use pliers to trim away all but ⅜in (9mm) of six upholstery nails. Use an uncut nail to pierce a hole in the centre of each gold shape. Spread Superglue on the back of the trimmed nail, and push into the hole. Repeat with the other nails. When dry, coat the bangle with varnish.

5 Earrings: Cut thin card into two 1¼in (3cm) squares. Cut a large compressed paper ball in half and use PVA to stick half a ball centrally on each card square. When dry, turn card over and use Superglue to stick an earring clip to the back of each square. Leave to dry.

6 Paste very small strips of newspaper over ball and card, until the front and glued clip backs are completely covered. Leave to dry.

7 Holding an earring by its clip, paint with an undercoat, and when dry, paint with grey metallic paint. When dry colour-in round the square with gold, and paint gold spots on the ball. Trim a nail as for the bangle, and attach to the centre of the ball in the same way. Varnish all over. Finish the other earring to match.

8 Necklace: Use a large darning needle to pierce a hole through each paper ball, including a large ball. Paint the balls with grey metallic paint, and leave to dry (see Better Papercrafts). Apply a second coat

and leave to dry. Decorate the balls with gold spots. On the large ball, colour-in a large gold circle round the hole. Leave to dry.

9 Add 4 upholstery nails to the large ball as for the other jewellery pieces. Varnish all the balls. Knot the thread end to half of the necklace fastening. Thread on one gold bead, a paper bead, a gold bead and so on, placing the large bead at the centre. Continue threading gold beads and paper beads. Knot the thread end securely to the other necklace fastening. Pass the thread ends back down through the beads for 3in (7.5cm), trim thread ends to neaten.

1 **Bow jewellery:** Draw the bow shapes on to corrugated card. Cut with scissors.

2 Wrap very small pasted strips over the card, taking care to fold paper neatly over the points. To make the centre knots, scrunch a small piece of pasted paper into a ball, and stick in position. Hold in place with small pasted strips stuck criss-cross over the top. Leave to dry. Colour the fronts and backs of the bows with gold marker.

3 **Bowed bangle:** Make the bangle following stages 1–2 for the pewter and gold bangle. Colour, substituting gold for grey paint.

4 Decorate the right sides of bows and bangles using a glitter pen.

5 Use black paint and a very fine, almost dry watercolour brush to mark in shadows, and cloth fold effects (see picture). Colour-in each edge of the bangle with black. Varnish when dry.

6 Use Superglue to stick a small bow to the bangle. Glue jewellery findings to the backs of other bows.

Pleated jewellery

Paper can be folded concertina-style and squeezed into shape to make all kinds of attractive and unusual jewellery.

Materials

Artist's Canson paper in two colours
Toning giftwrap paper
Spray adhesive, PVA, Superglue, clear
  craft glue
Craft knife, straight cutting edge
Set square, small nosed pliers
Small rubber bands
You will also need:
For the earrings: Straight eye wires and
  earring findings
For the brooch: A small hole punch,
  small beads with a hole diameter large
  enough to take narrow ribbon or cord,
  a brooch or lapel pin

Preparation

1 To prepare the base layer, cut a strip of artist's paper 3in (7.5cm) deep and about 7in (18cm) long. Mark this measurement with a set square to ensure edges are at right angles. Gently tear the paper along one long edge, so that the layered part of the tear is on the underside of the paper. From patterned giftwrap cut a strip the same size as the base layer. Tear along one long edge in the same way. Place it over the base layer, the torn layer underneath should be visible. Tear away some more if necessary. Spray the back of the giftwrap with adhesive and stick over the base layer. Cut the top plain layer to the same width, but to half the depth of the other layers. Tear as before, and stick in place. Trim the top and side edges through all layers if necessary. Leave to dry.

2 Pleat into concertina pleats ¼in (6mm) wide. On the right side, the first pleat should face down. If the last pleat does not face the same way as the first trim the end to match.

1 Earrings: Each earring is made from a prepared section 2½in (6cm) deep and 3½in (9cm) wide. Prepare the paper layers and pleat. Protect the pleated length with PVA by diluting PVA to a creamy consistency. Paint over the surface with a fine watercolour brush. Leave to dry. Dab a little clear adhesive between each pleat back and front, and press to stick. Insert a straight wire attached to an earring hook between the centre pleats. Trim the straight wire if necessary to prevent it showing where pleats fan out. Apply a little Superglue to the wire. Hold in place with a small rubber band round the pleats. Leave to dry.

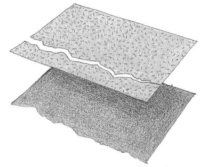

Tear the gift paper so that the layered edge is on the underside. Place on the torn, grey, artist's paper

Pleat the three-layered piece into ¼in (6mm) concertina pleats. The first and last pleats should face down

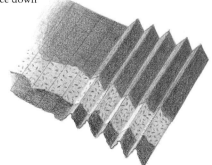

2 Fold a narrow strip of patterned giftwrap and glue round the pleats. Overlap at back and trim. Repeat with the other earring.

3 Brooch: Pleat a prepared strip in the same way as for the earrings, but trim the top edge so that the depth of the pleats is 1¾in (4.5cm). Trim the strip to eleven pleats. Punch a small hole through the top of each pleat, ⅛in (3mm) from the edge. Protect with PVA as for earrings. Thread a narrow ribbon through the holes, and pull up length to make an open fan shape. Thread a small bead on each side of the fan and pull the ribbon up tightly. Hold the fan closed with a rubber band and tie a knot in the ribbon outside each bead. Remove the rubber band. Thread the ribbon ends through a third bead. Remove the rubber band and tie in a knot to secure. Trim the ribbon ends level. Stick a brooch pin to the back of the fan with Superglue.

By changing the colours of the papers you can create quite different effects. Try making up the designs in bright hot shades, or cool pale pastels, and you will see how versatile pleated jewellery can be.

FOUR

Toys and Origami

Origami boxes

Origami – the Japanese art of paper folding – has been popular for hundreds of years. These classic designs are made from a basic square of paper. You can vary the finished effect by changing the size of the square, and by working two paper squares together as a contrast. Use the boxes to present gifts and sweets, or to hold small stationery items.

Materials

Pre-cut squares of Origami paper, or thin art paper such as Ingres paper or giftwrap. (Choose any paper which takes a crease easily. Start by working on a single 10in (25cm) practice square of thin copy paper.)
Stick adhesive

PLEATED DIAMOND BOX

This box has a pleated diamond shaped top edge, and stands on four triangular shaped feet.

Preparation

1 Cut 2 paper squares to the required size. Place both sheets together, wrong sides facing and secure at the centre with a small dab of adhesive. Smooth flat. Crease diagonally both ways as shown.

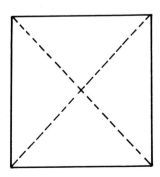

2 Fold the corners to the centre.

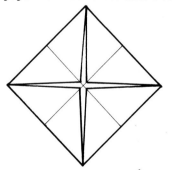

3 The paper now looks like this. Turn it over.

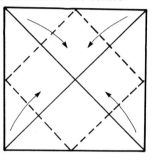

4 Fold the corners to the centre.

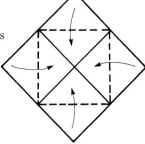

5 Fold over the points as shown.

6 The piece now looks like this. Turn it over.

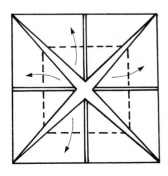

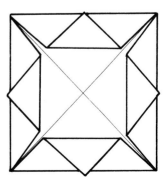

61

7 Fold the flaps into pleats by creasing in the opposite direction as shown.

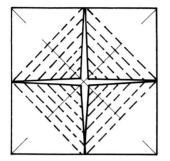

8 This shows the pleated effect.

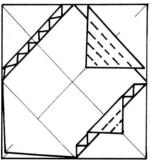

9 Push your thumb into the corners to lift the shape. Press the sides together on the outside to shape.

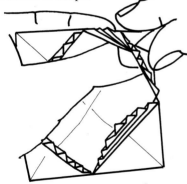

10 The completed box. The contents will weight the box down to hold it in shape.

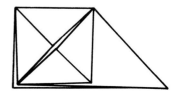

FLAPPED BOX

This box has a square base and side flaps. Work a set in different sizes and in co-ordinating papers.

1 Crease the square diagonally.

2 Fold the corners to the centre.

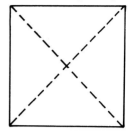

3 Turn over. Fold in half.

4 Squash the top down to flatten.

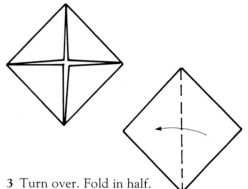

5 Flattened top section. Turn over.

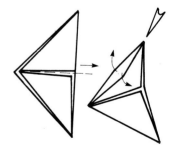

6 Lift the flap up.

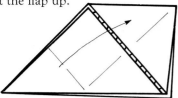

7 Squash the top down to flatten.

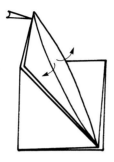

8 Ease open the flaps.

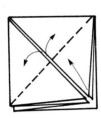

9 Squash the flaps flat. Turn over.

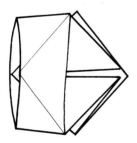

10 Repeat with the flaps on this side.

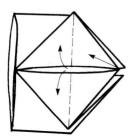

11 Move the left section behind, and the right section forward.

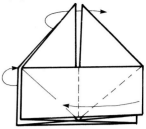

12 Fold to centre. Repeat on the other side.

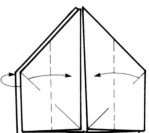

13 Fold the flap down. Repeat on the other side.

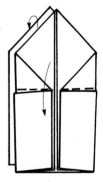

14 Ease the sides down to complete the box.

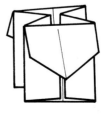
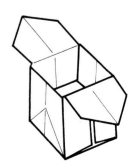

Spotty dog

Amuse your friends with this playful dog, whose appealing expression and floppy ears are sure to capture their hearts. You can make the mask complete with bone, or as a simplified version – just add a tongue.

Materials

Dressmakers' squared paper, scale
  1sq = 1in (2.5cm)
Thin white card
Two shades of brown Canson paper,
  dark for ears and chin, light for eye
  patch
Black paper, black sticky-back velour for
  nose
Two shades of pink art paper – dark for
  tongue, light for lip
Two shades of grey art paper, mid grey
  for bone, dark grey for upper lip/nose
  line
Cream paper for teeth
Hole punch and wad punch
Round hat elastic
Two self adhesive pads
Spray adhesive, double sided sticky tape

Preparation

1 Draw patterns from the graph patterns
on pages 66–67. Take a tracing to use as a
guide when positioning the mask details.
Transfer the mask front pattern to thin
card and cut out. Score lightly and fold
along the tops of the ears.

2 Trace the ear shapes on to dark brown
paper, cut out and stick in place, level
with the fold line. Cut out the patch and
stick in place. Cut out the grey lip line
and stick in place.

3 Punch the muzzle spots from dark
brown paper and stick in place. Cut out 2
black eye circles, and the dark brown
eyebrows. Cut a nose from black velour
stuck to black paper. Stick 2 adhesive
pads on the back of the nose shape and
stick the nose on the mask. Leave the
mask at this stage if you wish, and add a
tongue, glued behind the muzzle.

Mask backing

4 Transfer the mask backing pattern to
white card and cut out. Cut out all other
shapes from paper as outlined on the
pattern.

5 Using the tracing to help you place the
shapes, stick the brown chin shape in
place, and stick the tongue over this. Cut
out the teeth and lip shapes and stick the
lip over the teeth. Stick the lip in place
making sure the teeth remain free.

6 Cut out the bone. Lay the bone
between the teeth, and secure by placing
a little double sided sticky tape behind
the bone.

Assembling the mask

7 Open the mask front flat, and avoiding
the ears (mask these off with a spare piece
of paper) spray the back with adhesive.
Lay the mask over the mask backing, and
ease the teeth to the front of the mask.
Leave to dry.

8 Use the wad punch to cut holes for
eyes and holes for the elastic. Measure
the elastic to reach round the head,
thread through the holes and tie in a knot
at the back.

DOG MASK FRONT
Cut 1 from white card/paper

1 sq = 1 inch (2.5cm)

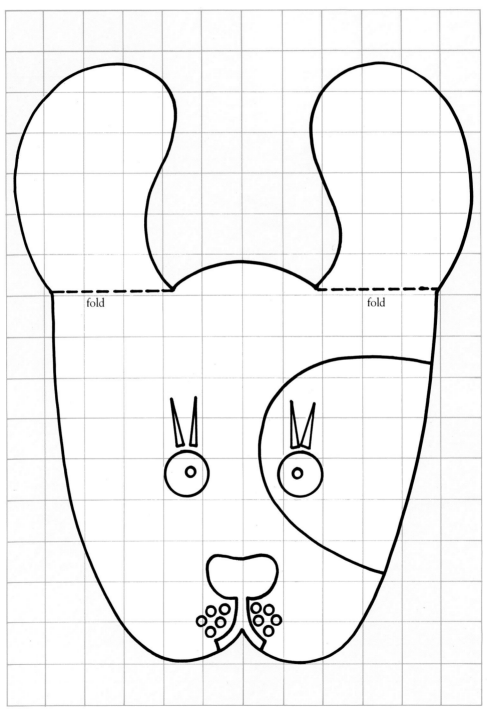

fold

fold

MASK BACKING
Cut outline shape from white card/paper

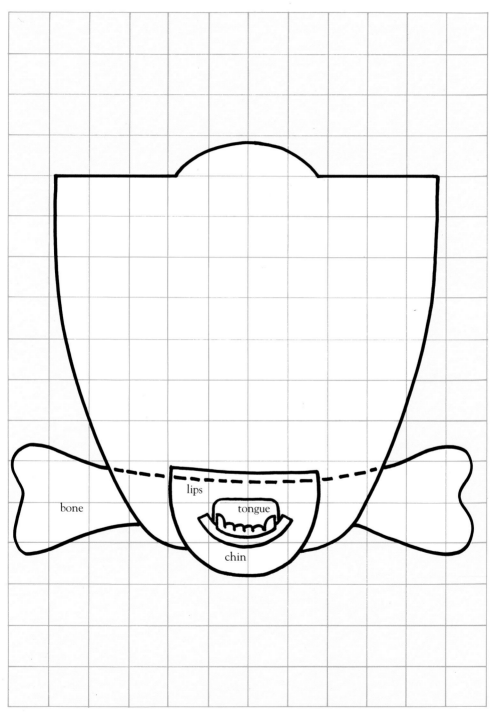

bone

lips

tongue

chin

Flower mobile

Scribble-coloured flowers create this easy-to-make mobile. Made from cartridge paper and hung from wires they are child's play!

Materials

Cartridge paper
Mobile wires: one 10½in (27cm) long, two
    7½in (19cm) long
Felt tipped pens (seven colours)
Stick adhesive
Invisible thread, sewing needle, sticky
    tape

Making the flowers

1 Make a tracing of the half flower shape
and retrace to make a template. Cut out 2
shapes for each flower from cartridge
paper. Crease lightly along the fold lines
and cut along one line to the centre. Cut
out 14 shapes (7 flowers).

2 Use felt tipped pens, and refer to the
picture as a guide to colour the flowers
with simple one-stroke marks. Colour a
flower centre and then work round the
outsides of the petals. To help balance
the final effect, try to introduce a touch
of all 7 colours on each flower.

3 To shape a flower, spread adhesive
over the triangular section marked 'cut'.
Fold the flower into shape by pressing
the glued area under the adjoining
triangle. To complete the flower, spread
adhesive on the back of each scallop edge
of one flower shape, and join to another
flower shape, matching overlap points.
Press together to stick, and trim the edges
level to neaten if necessary.

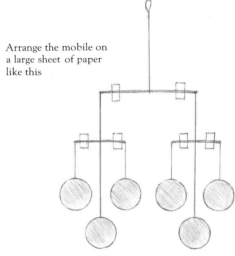

Arrange the mobile on
a large sheet of paper
like this

Trace-off pattern for the flower

place to fold

fold   cut

fold   fold   fold   fold   fold

fold   fold

**Trace-off pattern
for the leaves**

Cut 2 for each flower

68

Assembling the mobile

4 Secure the largest mobile wire with sticky tape to a large sheet of paper or a smooth work surface. Lay short wires about 7½in (18cm) below this, with the end points of the large wire level with the centres. Secure with sticky tape. Take a length of invisible thread and securely tie a piece 15in (38cm) long to the mid-point of the large wire. Tie a loop at the other end to hang the mobile.

5 Pierce a needle through the flower scallop at the overlapping point and thread a short length of thread through this. Secure by knotting. Place a flower 3in (7.5cm) below the centre of the wire. Secure the thread position with sticky tape and knot the end to the wire. Join flowers to the small wires, positioning each one 3in (7.5cm) from the wire ends, securing the position with sticky tape as

before. Hang a flower from the centre point of each short wire, positioning each one 10in (25cm) from the centre of the wire.

6 Adding leaves: Make a tracing of the leaf pattern and cut a template. Cut out 14 leaf shapes. Colour one side of each. Spread adhesive on the wrong side of one leaf, and attach to the wrong side of another leaf. Check the fit of the pair and trim as necessary. Spread adhesive on the wrong side of one leaf, slip the leaf pair round the thread, just above the flower, and press leaves together to stick. Repeat with all flowers.

Hanging the mobile

7 Remove the sticky tapes carefully, and hang the mobile where it will catch the draught – under a light fitting, or near a window.

FIVE

Greetings

Treasure bags

These little woven containers are so simple to make and are ideal for holding small gifts or sweets.

Materials

Strong, coloured paper, or laminate giftwrap to cartridge paper for the container base

Contrast papers (prepared to equal weight) for weaving

Clear craft glue

1 To make the base, follow the diagram. Cut a rectangle 6¼ × 3in (16 × 7.5cm) from paper. Draw a line ¼in (6mm) all round inside the outline. Within this, measure and mark lines ½in (12mm) apart. Cut along the lines with a craft knife. Fold the paper in half across its width.

2 Cut 6 strips of contrast paper, each ½in (12mm) wide, and long enough to wrap round the bag with a generous overlap. With the base folded, weave one strip across the next to the fold line. Continue weaving across the back. Weave in the

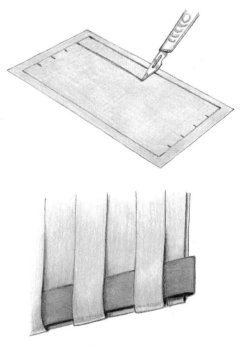

Cut long strips of contrast paper and weave them round the folded base piece

Draw this diagram on strong, coloured paper

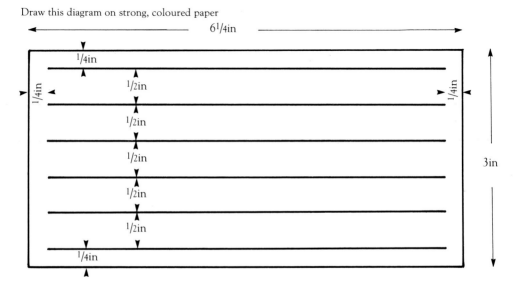

ends securely into the inside and outside of the bag. Trim the excess strip so that the ends do not show on the outside. Continue weaving in the same way with 4 more strips.

Handle

3 To make the handle, cut the remaining strip to 8in (20cm) long and weave each end into the pattern at the centre on the insides of the bag. Secure with glue.

Surprises in store

These cone boxes are ideal for jewellery and other small special gifts. Folded to shape from one piece of card, they are quick to make and a pleasure to decorate with colourful scraps and trims.

Materials
Thin card
Giftwrap paper
Spray adhesive
Clear craft glue
Victorian paper scraps or other trims
Cord for loops
Small wad punch

Making the boxes
1 Trace the full-sized pattern on pages 76–77, joining lines where indicated with arrows. Trace shape on to card. Cut around the outline and crease along the fold lines. Bend the cone into shape.

2 Flatten the shape, and spray the right side with adhesive. Press on to giftwrap paper, smooth flat and cut round the card edges. Pierce a hole through the centre of the lid. Re-crease along the fold lines to shape the box.

3 Spread adhesive along the side flap and press to stick. Thread a loop of cord through the hole in the lid and knot on the underside. Stick a decorative scrap or trim on the box front.

4 To fasten the lid closed, stick a little double-sided sticky tape on the right side of the lid flaps. Remove the protective paper when the gift is inside, and seal by placing the flaps inside the box.

Spray the card with adhesive, press on a piece of gift paper

Glue the side flap and form the cone. Knot a cord loop through the lid hole

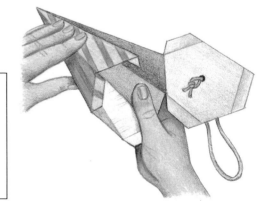

Make the boxes in seasonal colours to hang as decorations or special favours on the Christmas tree. Decorate the fronts with baubles or scraps of winter greenery and berries and fill with sweets, nuts or candied fruits.

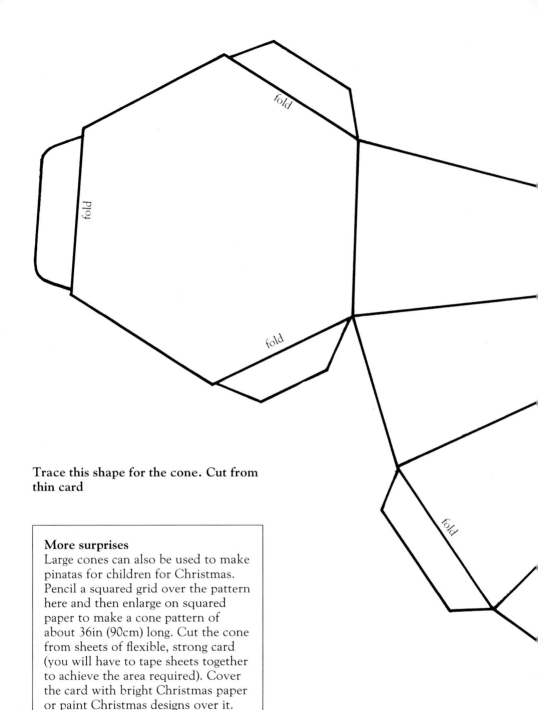

Trace this shape for the cone. Cut from thin card

More surprises

Large cones can also be used to make pinatas for children for Christmas. Pencil a squared grid over the pattern here and then enlarge on squared paper to make a cone pattern of about 36in (90cm) long. Cut the cone from sheets of flexible, strong card (you will have to tape sheets together to achieve the area required). Cover the card with bright Christmas paper or paint Christmas designs over it. Fill the cone with small gifts and hang it high on the wall or over a doorway. During the party, children are given thin sticks and encouraged to beat the pinata until it opens and showers them with gifts.

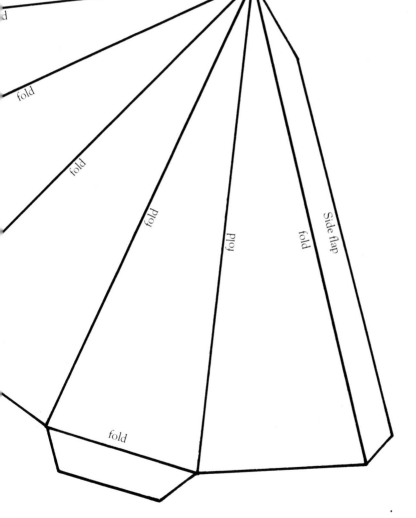

fold

fold

fold

fold

fold

fold

Side flap

fold

Cat and mouse

These popular pets make perfect greetings cards, and their appealing expressions are easy to achieve with the help of toymaking accessories.

Materials
For both designs:
Spray adhesive and clear craft glue
Sharp sewing needle
For the cat:
Orange Canson paper
White cartridge paper
Scrap of pink paper
Six black toy whiskers
2 cat eyes and one nose
Two self-adhesive pads
Black felt tipped pen (or black crayon)
For the mouse:
Dark grey Canson paper
Pink Canson paper
Scrap of black sticky-backed velour (or black paper)
6in (15cm) length of very narrow pale pink ribbon
Six transparent plastic whiskers
2 small goggly eyes
Scrap of white paper
One self-adhesive pad

THE CAT
Preparation
1 Trace the cat pattern on pages 80–81, joining lines where indicated with arrows. Draw a line on a sheet of orange paper, score gently and fold in half. Place the fold to the fold line on the cat tracing. Cut through both thicknesses. Trace the head separately and cut out from a single thickness of paper.

2 Trace and cut out the head and body markings from white paper. Spray the backs of the pieces with adhesive, and position on cat shape using the tracing as a guide. Cut out a pink tongue and stick in place. Draw claws on cat's paws.

3 Use a needle to pierce holes for whiskers. Insert each whisker from the back, trimming off any plastic end pieces. Arrange the whiskers so they lay flat and are evenly spaced. Secure the whiskers at the back with a scrap of orange paper stuck over the whisker ends. Trim the whiskers to the desired length.

4 Stick the eyes and nose in place.

5 Using the tracing as a guide, place two adhesive pads on the body where the head overlaps, and position the head over these.

Draw the cat's body only on the folded orange card. The head is cut separately

Secure the mouse whiskers on the wrong side with strips of glued paper

THE MOUSE

6 Follow the basic instructions for tracing the mouse pattern (pages 80–81) and cut the mouse body from folded grey paper, and head from a single layer of grey paper. Cut out pink ears and glue behind head. Cut out a pink foot, and draw claws on it. Stick in place.

7 Stick the eyes in place. Pierce the face for the whiskers and insert them. Secure the whiskers with glued paper as for the cat. Snip teeth from white paper and stick in position. Stick the nose in place.

8 Pierce a small hole for the tail, and thread ribbon through. Knot on the wrong side.

9 Place an adhesive pad on the body behind the head area, and stick the head in place.

Trace these patterns for the Cat and Mouse

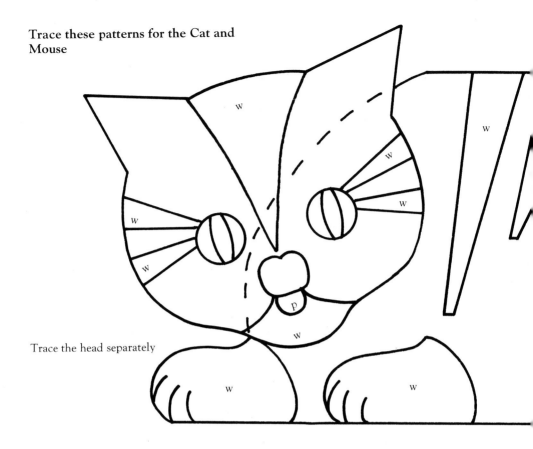

Trace the head separately

Cat calendar

The cat card can be adapted to make an amusing calendar. Construct the cat on a single piece of orange paper. Cut the same shape from orange paper twice more and mount the finished cat on double-sided adhesive pads, as described for the 3-D découpage cards on page 86. You might also lift forward the cat's head and paws in the same way. Cut a rectangle of stiff card and cover it with gift-wrap paper. Glue the cat to the upper half of the card and a calendar block to the lower half. You can either make a strut for the back so that the calendar stands up or a ribbon hanger can be glued behind the top edge.

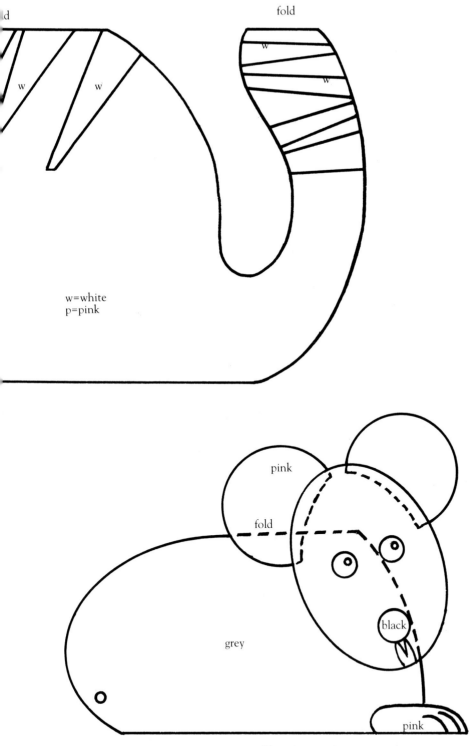

fold

w

w

w

w

w=white
p=pink

pink

fold

black

grey

pink

Carried away

A tote bag is an ever popular, versatile container – the ideal solution for wrapping an awkwardly shaped gift, and attractive enough to keep as a lightweight holdall for all kinds of miscellaneous materials.

Materials

Decorative giftwrap paper (or patterned wallpaper)
Cartridge paper (or wall lining paper)
Thin card
Spray adhesive
Stick adhesive
Cord or ribbon for handles
String for gift tags
Hole punch

Making tote bags

A tote bag can be any size you wish to make, simply by adapting the basic pattern and following one basic rule: the depth of the base overlap sections on the bag (marked on pattern **A** plus half again) should always measure more than half the depth (marked **A**) of each tote side. All **A** measurements should be equal, so that the bag holds its shape well and folds flat. By simply checking these proportions you can make professional looking tote bags, from mini totes to maxi sizes. When making large bags, join papers at each side so that the joins do not show.

Making the lining

1 Following the diagram (on page 84), draw the tote measurements on to a sheet of cartridge (or a similar weight of paper). Cut out. Starting with the main vertical lines, crease the fold lines to shape. Crease the base line and the fold line which runs across the back section. Carefully crease the side triangular shaped sections. Next, fold the side lines together, and pinch the triangles into place. Open out again.

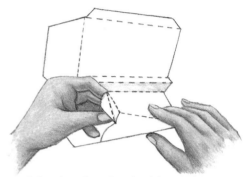

Spread glue along the right side of the side flap, press to the inside edge of the tote side

With one hand inside as a support, press the flaps together to stick

Press the base section along the crease lines

Covering the lining

2 Lay the cartridge paper flat, creased side facing and spray with adhesive. Lay the covering paper flat wrong side facing, and press the cartridge, sticky side down, on to this. Position it so that there is an overlap of covering paper at the top edge of about 3in (7.5cm). Smooth flat on both sides of paper. Trim level with the cartridge edges, adjusting the top overlap size accurately if necessary. Fold along the creases to shape the paper smoothly.

3 Cut a reinforcing strip of thin card to the same depth as the overlap and as wide as the tote (excluding the side flap) and stick across the top of the cartridge paper. Spread adhesive underneath the top overlap and press flat to stick to the card strip.

4 Spread adhesive along the right side of the side flap, and press to the inside edge of the tote side. Align the edges, and top and base lines neatly. Press to stick.

5 Turn the bag upside down. Spread adhesive on the edges of the right sides of the base side flaps, and along the edge of the wrong side of the under flap. With one hand inside the bag as support, press the flaps together to stick, making sure that the bag keeps its shape. Now spread adhesive under the remaining base flap, and press to stick.

6 Smooth the tote bag edges, making sure that they are all aligned. Gently press the base section flat along the crease lines, so that the base rests flat against the bag.

The handles

7 Position the handles to suit the proportions of the bag. The holes for the handles are marked with a hole punch. To achieve a good balance, position these between a third to a quarter of the front width in from each side. Place the holes about ¾in (18mm) down from the top edge, or as far as the punch will reach, to avoid tearing the paper.

Diagram for the tote bag

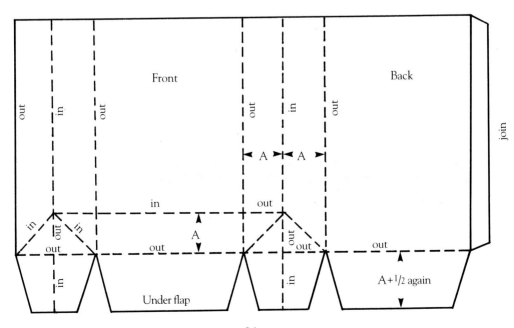

8 Make two handles – one on each side of the bag – or thread a long cord through all four holes and secure the ends with a knot on the inside (or tie in a bow). For each handle cut a length of cord or ribbon long enough to thread through both holes and provide a comfortable handle.

Gift tags

9 Make a gift tag to match or contrast with the tote bag. Laminate a piece of giftwrap to cartridge paper or thin card, and crease to mark a centre fold. Cut round to the shape required, and punch a hole near the fold to hold the tie. Alternatively, cut round the outline of a suitable motif and laminate this to paper or card.

3D découpage

This quick version of an increasingly popular craft uses motifs on giftwrap paper to create greeting cards with an added dimension. Specially selected areas are cut out and elevated with tiny sections cut from sticky adhesive pads to make the picture 'come alive'.

Materials
Four or five identical motifs from
  giftwrap, posters or notecards
Cartridge paper (optional)
Stiff paper or thin card for base
Spray adhesive
Double sided adhesive pads
Small manicure scissors with curved
  blades

Preparation
1 If you are using thin paper, laminate it to cartridge paper. Use the small scissors to cut out one complete design motif. Mount this on the base paper or card with spray adhesive. (Do not cut this to finished size yet.)

Working the design
2 Cover the whole design area with sticky pads, cutting them down to size as necessary. Avoid placing them at the edge of the design where they may show. Cut out another complete motif and position this accurately over the sticky pads.
3 Look at your chosen motif and decide which areas you want to lift forward, bearing in mind that the aim is to lift the subject matter in the foreground closer, so that details which appear closest to you in the picture will be the top layer of your design. Place sticky pads over your selected areas, and cut out the relevant details from the third motif. Stick these over the pads.

4 Continue adding sticky pads to the chosen areas, and cut more details from the fourth motif. Position over the pads.

If you are using a fifth motif, add these details over another layer of sticky pads in the same way.

5 When the design is complete, decide on the finished shape of the greetings card, to show the design off to best advantage. Mark the shape with a pencil and set square, and cut out with a craft knife. Fold to shape.

Cover the whole design area with sticky pads

Place sticky pads over selected areas ready to position the third layer of motifs

Paper lace

Sewing needles are all that is needed to transform a sheet of paper into an intricate piece of lace. Different effects are achieved by pricking along a drawn outline using various size needles, or by piercing from both sides of the paper. The results can be used to create a picture, or to personalize stationery and giftwraps with small motifs and borders.

Materials
Cartridge paper and another smooth, fairly stiff paper in a toning colour
Tracing paper
Padding: thick felt, blanket or folded cloth
Tapestry needle and a darning needle
Large eraser
Manicure scissors with curved blades
Set square, ruler, craft knife, sticky tape, spray adhesive

Preparation
1 Make a handle for the needles by embedding each one at opposite ends of the eraser. The larger needle is used to emphasize shapes, and the smaller needle is used and for less prominent shapes.

Basic techniques
2 Holes pierced from the wrong side of the paper have greater definition because of their high relief, while holes pierced from the right side are smooth and less obtrusive, so this can be used to give a sense of perspective to the design. Space the holes equally apart, and not too close together, otherwise the paper may tear. Try out effects with the needles on a spare piece of paper.

3 Trace the landscape (see pages 90–91) and the half border pattern on pages 92–93. Re-trace the half border on folded paper to obtain the complete border. Using two different coloured pencils,

trace the landscape design on to one sheet of tracing paper, and the complete border on to another. These tracings will be the working patterns.

4 Lay the cartridge paper on a flat surface, and then lay the tracing of the landscape, with the wrong side facing upwards over this. Attach with sticky tape placed along the top edge. Lay both sheets over the padded surface. Use the tapestry needle to prick out the outline of the large clouds, lamb and the cottage roof. Use the darning needle to prick the outline of the bushes and trees, birds and sun. Carefully remove the tracing paper.

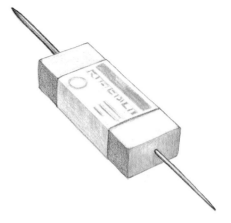

Make a handle for the needles by embedding them into opposite ends of an eraser

Paper lace gift card

Designs for paper lace gift cards can be traced from books, magazines, or from giftwrap or wallpapers. Mount the pricked paper on a bought gift card blank or make a card by cutting and folding coloured cartridge paper. It is a good idea to make your card to a standard envelope size.

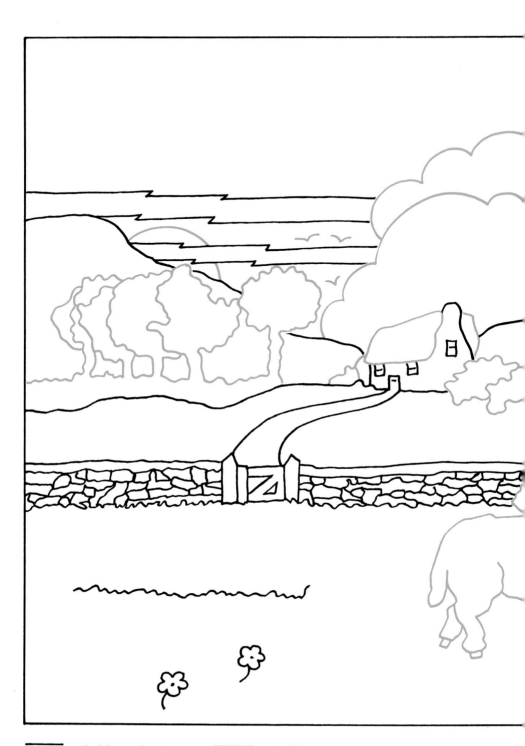

———— worked from right side ———— worked from reverse

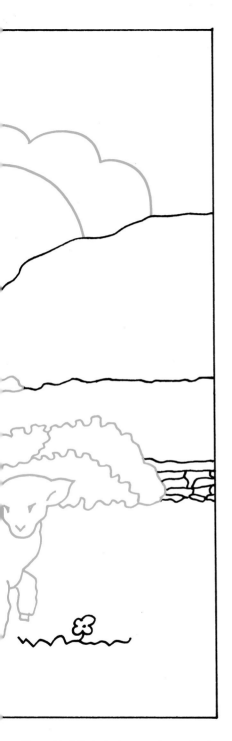

5 Turn the cartridge paper over and replace the tracing, carefully lining up the pricked holes. Prick out the rest of the landscape using the large needle to mark the wispy cloudline, the hills, path and top of the wall. Use the smaller needle to mark all the other details. Remove the tracing and set cartridge paper aside.

The border
6 Take a coloured sheet of paper, and using the border tracing as a guide, mark out the centre rectangle. Cut this away with a craft knife. Trim the paper around the rectangle to make a 2in (5cm) border all round. Spray the wrong side of border with adhesive, and position the border over the landscape, using the original tracing as a guide.

7 Place the landscape and border, wrong side facing upwards, to padded surface. Position the border tracing on top, lining up the outline carefully, and prick the design. Use the tapestry needle to mark the large flower outlines, and the straight band nearest the flowers. Use the darning needle to prick the smaller flowers and the leaves. Remove the tracing and turn the work over to the right side.

Trace this full-sized picture and use with the frame on pages 92–93

PAPER LACE BORDER

——————— worked from reverse   ——————— worked from reverse

centre fold

top

8 Re-position the tracing, and use the darning needle to prick out the inner straight band. Mark in the lines on the petals and small scroll shapes. Remove tracing. Carefully cut round the border outline (see broken line) with the curved scissors, cutting to within $\frac{1}{4}$in (6mm) of the pricked outlines. Frame the picture on a neutral colour background to complement the delicate effect.

inner edge

Ribbon box

Giftwrap ribbon can be woven and used as a decorative insert for a special giftbox.

Materials

Cartridge paper or copy paper
Giftwrap ribbon in six colours
Medium-weight card
Giftwrap paper, lining paper
Masking tape
Spray adhesive, clear craft glue

Preparation

1 Decide the area size you are going to weave. Cut the ribbons to a little more than the depth of the area. Tape the ribbons side by side vertically, on cartridge paper with the ends level, in a six-colour sequence to make the warp.

2 Keeping to the same colour sequence, weave the same number of ribbons in and out across the warp (these horizontal ribbons are called the weft). Tape the ends.

3 Use masking tape to mask off the design area, and cut out the woven square cutting through the centre of the securing tapes. Trim away paper underneath, so that weave is supported on the edges only by the tape. Place the work wrong side up and spray the back with adhesive. Press, sticky side down, on to another piece of cartridge and trim round.

Making the box

4 For this design, start by making the box lid, as this is custom-made to fit the woven insert. The lid is made from one piece of card. On card, draw the central square shape for the woven insert. To do this, measure and mark the size of the woven square within the masked area. Decide on size of surrounding lid, and mark this on to card. Extend edges to make box sides and add a flap at each end

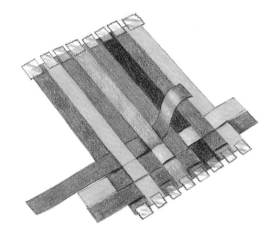

Tape the warp ribbons to paper, weave the weft ribbons in and out

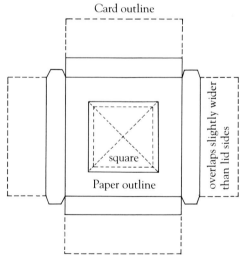

Box lid: Decide the size and draw out the lid square, extend the edges for the box sides, add a flap at the ends of the side pieces

of two side pieces. Cut out the central square and discard. Cut round the lid outline and gently score the fold lines round the lid top and for flaps.

5 Open the lid flat, and spray the scored side with adhesive. Press flat on to the wrong side of giftwrap. Cut out round the edge allowing an overlap on each side to reach round to inside the lid. Cut across the centre square diagonally, and turn back the paper. Trim and stick to the wrong side, and stick the side overlaps to the wrong side with clear adhesive. Spread adhesive on the side overlaps and press to the inside edges, then stick the paper overlaps in place as side linings.

6 Run a line of adhesive around the masking tape on the woven insert, and stick in place on the wrong side of the lid. Line the lid.

7 Make the box base. Measure the inside box lid, and draw a square a little smaller than the lid measurement on to card. This is the base. Extend the lines to the required depth, as for the lid, to make the box sides. Add flaps and score. Stick the box to paper and cover in the same way, allowing extra paper at the sides for overlaps and full linings.

SIX

Better Papercrafts

❧

Read this chapter before starting work on a project, as here you will find useful information about selecting the best paper for the job, what tools and equipment to use and how to prepare papers for special crafts like papier mâché and découpage.

Different papers

There is a wealth of paper and card to choose from, in a variety of weights and sizes. Artist's cover paper and rougher textured Canson paper are available in a good colour range, and they cut, curl and crease well. Among many uses these papers are ideal for paper weaving, making cards and jewellery, lining boxes and for collage decoration. Cartridge paper is drawing paper. Use this for design work as well as for making strong linings and backings to thinner papers. It is worth investing in an A2-size pad of cartridge paper as you can cut smaller pieces from this if needed.

Typing and copy paper fold and cut easily. These are invaluable for trying out designs, and patterns can be transferred to these for reference. Use good quality tracing paper for transferring designs and copying pattern shapes. An A3-size pad is practical for most needs. Refer to page 104.

Beautifully textured, special handmade papers like Japanese papers and some artist's papers are expensive, but usually one or two sheets of these are all that is needed for a project as you can use them frugally, choosing them to embellish rather than to create the basic design.

Tissue papers are available in a wide colour range. Good quality tissue is surprisingly strong. You will find it useful for decorating papier mâché as well as providing the perfect finishing touch to gift wrapping.

Craft papers

The flowermaking projects in this book both use double crêpe paper, available from specialist suppliers and craft shops. This is of double thickness as the name suggests, and is often available in a two-tone effect and so is ideal for creating petals. Crêpe paper is very stretchy, so take note of pattern instructions when placing pattern pieces and cutting out, to achieve the desired effect. Another popular craft paper is paper ribbon. This is often presented wound tightly in coils, so the ribbon has to be gently unfurled to the required width. Although designed for making bows and ties it can also be used for plaiting and weaving. The surface texture of paper ribbon also lends itself well to leaf making, as in the Evergreen garland project (see page 34).

Perhaps the most used paper in this book is giftwrap paper and the choice here is enormous. When choosing giftwrap for a project, check that it will fold and crease well without the surface colour cracking and flaking, or marking easily. Foil papers add sparkle, but some tend to be rather springy and difficult to manage. Use them in small amounts – perhaps for weaving and bead making.

Other papers used in projects include pages from glossy magazines. These tend to be thin, but as with other lightweight papers, they can be laminated to a thicker paper to make them more manageable. (See page 100 'Using spray adhesive', for how to do this.)

Artist's mounting card is the thickest card used for the projects. It cuts and folds easily, and can be used to make boxes and containers, folder covers, backing boards or picture mounts. Thin card – so thin it is almost thick paper – is sometimes available with a glossy surface. This is ideal for making small gift boxes and greetings cards, as the surface sheen is an added bonus. Choose white, as the coloured surface on thin card can flake unattractively. Other card used includes postal tubes and card cylinders.

When you are selecting card for a project, especially when making stationery items, look at similar designs on sale in the shops, to help guide your choice of thickness.

Handling paper
Paper falls into two main categories – handmade paper and machine-made paper. Most of the papers used in this book are machine-made. Rather like woven fabric, machine-made papers have a 'grain' to them, which is made as the fibres are dragged along in one direction during the manufacturing process. Handmade papers have no grain, as the paper sheets are made separately and the fibres settle in a random way. When you tear a piece of paper along its grain, the paper rips quite easily and the torn edge is fairly even. Paper torn across its grain leaves a jagged edge, which can be attractive, but it is more difficult to control the tear. These different qualities can be used to advantage, particularly for collage style decoration and papier mâché, where you can decide on the outline texture of the paper shapes. It is much easier to fold and cut a piece of paper along its grain than across it, especially when working with thicker

Paper torn along its grain rips easily and the edge is fairly even

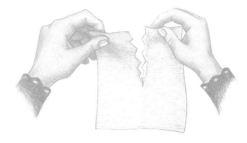

Paper torn across its grain leaves a jagged edge which can be attractive in some projects

papers, so note the grain direction when cutting out pattern shapes.

Tools and equipment
Most equipment required for papercrafts is readily available, and you will have most of it already. There are a few specialist tools, however, which provide for greater creative possibilities, and help to give papercraft items a more professional finish.

The work surface is important. This should be at a good working height, flat and stable. You will require a protective surface to use over the work top, to protect it from cuts and scratches when using craft knives. A sheet of thick card or board is a suitable protection but should be replaced frequently as the surface will become pitted from successive knife cuts. It is worth investing in a special cutting mat. This has a surface which 'heals itself' after every cut, and thus remains smooth, and will not distort subsequent cuts made over it.

GLOSSARY OF TERMS

Canson paper
This is a textured art paper, used for pastel drawing. It comes in about 20 shades.

Cartridge paper or construction paper
This comes in different weights and qualities in white only. *Cover paper* which is a similar weight comes in several colours.

Ingres paper
This is a thin art paper with a texture of thin lines. Available in a good colour range.

Corrugated card (railroad card)
This is available in two forms. In one, the corrugated surface is open to one side. In the other, the corrugations are enclosed between two smooth surfaces.

Brown paper (Kraft paper)
Ordinary brown, good quality parcel wrapping paper.

Mounting card (mount card)
Available in 3 qualities, 4, 6 and 8 sheet, 4 being the thinnest. It is available in a range of colours, including black and grey, all with a white back.

Shiny card
This is like a thin mounting card but with a coloured, shiny surface.

Wad punch
This has a straight handle and punches of different sizes fit into the end. The punch is placed over thick card and the end is tapped with a hammer. It enables a hole to be accurately placed.

Stationery punch
These operate on a spring. Some can punch 2 holes and others a single hole.

Scoring
Breaking the surface of card or thick paper with a knife tip to enable a sharper fold to be made.

Laminating
In the context of this book, spraying the surface of card or paper with adhesive, then applying a thinner paper to the surface.

Cut straight lines aligning the knife against a metal rule

Cutting tools
You will need two kinds of craft knives: a heavy duty knife, like a Stanley knife or an X-acto knife, for cutting thick card, and a small knife, preferably a scalpel, for thin card and paper. Use straight blades, as these suit most tasks, and replace them often for the best results. Needless to say, these knives require care when in use. You should always cut straight lines by lining up the knife against a firm straight edge. Use a metal rule for this rather than a plastic or wood ruler, as these materials can easily catch in the blade.

Using spray adhesive

This very useful adhesive is ideal in projects which use giftwrap papers. An important advantage over other adhesives is its delayed sticking time, which means that sprayed papers can be re-positioned if necessary. Use spray adhesive to make thin papers more durable by laminating them to a thicker paper like cartridge paper. When laminating very small paper shapes, the spraying can be done with the paper resting on an expanse of newspapers. However it is best to make a spray booth from a cardboard carton, as this will protect surrounding surfaces and furnishings. Choose a carton large enough to comfortably hold the work for spraying.

Place a large box on its side and surround it with old newspapers. Place the card or paper shape as far inside as possible. To spray, hold the can upright and spray evenly over the surface with a sweeping motion. Handle the sticky work as little as possible when transferring it to the work surface. Lay the work sticky side up, and press the corresponding paper piece over. Smooth to stick, then trim round the shape as necessary. Turn over and smooth the surface flat.

You will need several pairs of sharp scissors. Have a pair of fairly small, easy-to-handle scissors with straight pointed blades for most cutting jobs, a longer broad-bladed pair for general cutting and stretching paper, and manicure scissors with curved blades for cutting round intricate shapes. A pair of tweezers is useful for handling small cutout shapes.

Other cutting tools mentioned in the book are punches. Besides belt punches and stationery punches, wad punches can be used to punch holes through paper or card. These metal tools have removable punch fittings with different diameter holes. The tool is placed in position on the card or paper and struck smartly with a hammer to pierce the surface. Wad punches have the advantage over scissor style punches in that you can position them freely, and the size range of punch fittings gives flexibility for design. These are inexpensive, and available by mail order (see page 112).

Other equipment

Precise paper folding and creasing is important. One really useful specialist tool for marking fold lines on paper is a bookbinder's bone folder, which looks rather like a small modelling tool. This is drawn along against a straight edge and leaves a gentle groove ready for folding. You can improvise, however, by using a knitting needle or a blunt, curve-bladed table knife, a letter opener or any other tool which creases rather than pierces the paper surface.

Drawing aids required include a pair of compasses, a set square and a ruler with

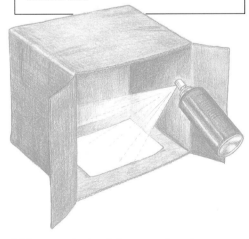

Make a spraying booth from a cardboard carton

To keep the nozzle of spray adhesive from clogging up after use, hold the can nozzle down and spray until the spray stops, then wipe over to clean the outside. If the spray has already clogged, wipe over with a cotton bud dipped in nail polish remover, then, if necessary, repierce the hole with a needle point.

Mark fold lines with a bookbinder's bone folder

small measurement markings, plus paper clips, and a stapler. You also need a pencil sharpener and a selection of HB and soft pencils, coloured pencils and felt tipped pens. A good quality eraser is essential.

Carbon paper is useful for transferring designs, but as the traced outlines cannot be removed, only use well-used carbon paper for tracings where the remaining outline does not matter.

Paints

Paints used for papercraft include poster paints, acrylics, water colours and designer gouache. You can also use household emulsion paints and model maker's enamel paints, as well as multi-purpose metallic paint. Varnish for finishing and protecting work can be gloss, satin or matt finish. Use a varnish suitable for paper, or a household varnish applied to the previously protected surface (see below). Paint brushes should include a range of watercolour brushes, and small household decorating brushes.

A spray fixative can be used to protect finished work. This leaves a protective sheen on the paper, making it less likely to mark or stain. Fixative can also be used on lightweight papers and paper printed on both sides – like magazine pages – to protect them from becoming

If you are constantly using a tube of quick-drying glue for a project, choose a nail which fits tightly into the nozzle and knock it through a small piece of hardboard. When not in use, place the nozzle of the tube over the nail. This seals it temporarily and the glue is ready to use when you need it.

transparent through over-wetting with glue or varnish.

Adhesives and tapes

Choose the right adhesive tape for the job. You may require transparent sticky tape, double-sided sticky tape, masking tape, or gummed brown paper tape. Specialist tapes like stretchy flowermaking tape (gutta tape) are available for binding wires and stems.

PVA is a multi-purpose, easy-to-use adhesive, which can be used both as a glue and a varnish. Although white, PVA dries transparent and gives a glossy protective surface. It can be used full strength or diluted with water. Clear, quick-drying and non-trailing craft glue (UHU) is a good multi-purpose adhesive for card and paper. Use a glue spreader for an even coverage. Stick adhesive (Pritt Stick) is required for some paper projects. This type of adhesive comes in a roll-up tube and is easy to control. An advantage is that unlike most other adhesives, it does not dampen the paper. Superglues are used to bond different types of material together. Use these for joining metal to paper for instance, as when attaching jewellery findings. One of the most useful adhesives, and probably the most widely used throughout the book, is spray adhesive. This allows you to laminate large or very small areas of paper together without stretching or dampening the paper. Spray adhesive should be used in a confined space to prevent the sticky mist settling on surrounding surfaces.

Cutting paper and card

To cut thick card, lay it flat on a protective surface. Draw the pattern outline directly on to the card. Use a set square and ruler to check right angles and parallel lines. Line up the straight metal edge against the line to be cut. Press the craft knife against the metal edge, and firmly draw the knife towards you, keeping an even pressure on the straight edge to keep it still. Score the cutting line gently to mark it (and if only marking fold lines) then still with the straight edge in position, cut along the line again, pressing harder to cut through the card. To cut round curves, mark the shape lightly with the knife point, and cut round making sure that the free hand is pressing firmly on the card to keep it still, and that fingers are not in line with the knife, should it slip.

To use a scalpel on paper, follow the same basic process. When cutting small shapes with right angles and tight curves, start by piercing the corner point of each shape with the point of the blade, and cut away from the corner, drawing the knife towards you. This should ensure neatly cut points.

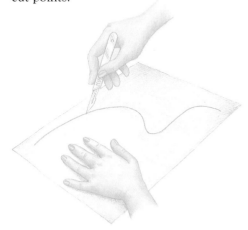

To cut round curves, mark the shape lightly with the knife point

When using scissors to cut paper shapes it is sometimes desirable to soften the cut edge, particularly with thick paper and when cutting shapes for

When cutting small shapes with a scalpel, start by piercing the corner point, then cut towards you

découpage, where the paper edge should be as thin and unobtrusive as possible. To do this, hold the paper right side facing you and roughly cut round the required shape, leaving a generous border round the main subject matter. Now hold the scissor blades at a slight angle away from you, and cut round again at the required edge. By cutting the paper at an angle you create a bevelled edge, making the harsh cutting line less noticeable. Use curved manicure scissors, the blades positioned appropriately, to cut out very small shapes.

Covering corners

Whether covering folder sides or boxes you can achieve neat, professional looking corners by following one of these methods. The first, folded method is more suitable for thin papers. The second, cut and dart method can be used for thicker papers, as bulk is reduced, and it gives neat covered corners on the edges of thick card, where it is sometimes difficult to avoid the card from showing through. However, if this does ever happen you can insert a little patch of matching paper over the corner, underneath the covering paper. Both of these methods use either a stick adhesive or a clear quick-drying craft glue to secure the corners and overlaps.

Folded corners

Working on the reverse of the card,

crease the overlap diagonally at the corner as shown, and stick the overlap on to the card. Crease the folded paper gently at the card edge and fold each overlap on to the card. Glue in place.

Cut and dart corners

Working on the reverse of the card, make a cut in line with each straight edge as shown then cut a narrow strip within that, tapering towards the corner of the card. Cut the overlaps (shaded areas on the diagram) away at each side. Gently apply glue to the centre strip, and smooth it on to the card. Press the strip flat to mould to the corner shape. Spread glue on the shaped overlaps, and press on to the card.

Stretching and curling paper

Paper grain can be used to advantage for moulding paper to a required shape. One of the easiest ways to shape paper is to gently stretch and curl it over a scissor blade. Papers that respond well to this are Canson and cover papers, cartridge and most lightweight papers, as well as crêpe paper and paper ribbon. To stretch the paper cut out the shape with the grain running in the direction to be stretched. Hold the paper in one hand and the open scissors blade in the other. Gently pull the blade across the underside of the paper, from the base to the tip of the shape. Repeat until the paper is curled sufficiently.

To stretch crêpe paper across its grain, to mould it into a rounded curve as for making flower petals, cut out the

Folded corner: Crease the overlap diagonally on the corner (left) then crease and fold the overlap on to the card (right)

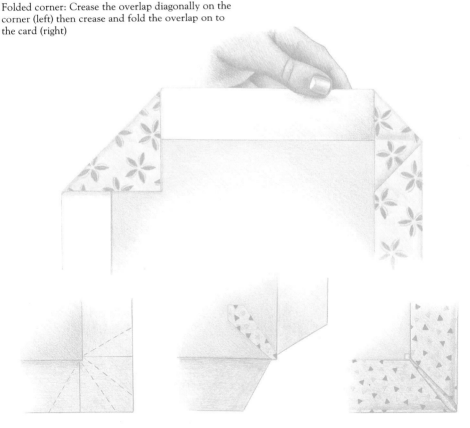

Cut and dart corner: Cut the overlaps away at each side (left).
Glue the centre strip on to the card (middle) then glue overlaps

Gently pull the blade across the underside of the paper until the paper curls

After cupping a flower petal, shape the edges by curling them over a scissor blade

required shape with the grain running opposite to the required stretch direction. Hold each side of the shape between thumb and fingers, and gently stretch, stroking the paper sideways with the thumbs to mould it. The upper and lower edges of the shape can be further shaped by curling over a scissors blade if required.

Pleating paper

Concertina pleats are equal size pleats, and are used in three projects in this book. The pleats are easy to make, relying on careful measuring and accurate folding. Cut a strip of paper to the required depth. Use a set square to check the right angle at one end of the strip and a ruler and pencil to measure and mark out equally spaced divisions along the

top and lower edge. Join these marks up with a ruler and pencil, then gently score along each line. Fold up the pleats. To join pleats, simply overlap the ends by an entire pleat, arranging the join so that the edge on the right side is hidden in the valley of the fold. Secure behind with adhesive.

Join the pleat marks with pencil and ruler, then score each line

PAPER AND BOARD SIZES

Traditional

Demy	$17\frac{1}{2} \times 22\frac{1}{2}$in ($444 \times 572$mm)
Medium	$18 \times 23\frac{1}{2}$in (457×584mm)
Royal	20×25in (508×636mm)
Imperial	22×30in (558×762mm)
Double	
Elephant	27×40in (686×1016mm)
Antiquarian	36×54in (914×1372mm)

International

A1	21×32in (525×800mm)
A2	$16\frac{1}{2} \times 23\frac{1}{2}$in (approx) 420×594mm
A3	$11\frac{1}{2} \times 16\frac{3}{4}$in (approx) 297×420mm
A4	$8\frac{1}{4} \times 11\frac{1}{2}$in (approx) 210×297mm
A5	$5\frac{3}{4} \times 8\frac{1}{4}$in (approx) 148×210mm

Board

Imperial	32×21in (813×533mm)
Double	
Imperial	44×32in (1118×813mm)
A1	$33\frac{1}{8} \times 23\frac{3}{8}$in ($841 \times 594$mm)
A0	$46\frac{3}{4} \times 33\frac{1}{8}$in ($1188 \times 841$mm)

Papier mâché

Papier mâché, which literally means 'chewed paper', can be worked in various ways. The projects in this book are all made using small strips of glue-soaked paper. Strips are overlapped and arranged over a mould (which can be anything from a bowl to a banana), until the layers are thick enough to hold the shape. This is usually possible after six or eight layers have been added. The work is left to dry completely, and is then removed from the mould, ready to be decorated. Old newspapers are a traditional favourite for providing the strips, as these are readily available, cost nothing, and are easy to handle. Decorative papers can be added as a final decoration, or if preferred, to make the entire object. The instructions here are for working the basic papier mâché strip technique over a mould. In projects follow individual project instructions for special details relating to those particular designs.

Basic technique

If using moulds to make an open object like a dish or bowl, the mould should be a shape which allows for easy removal of the finished papier mache. Avoid moulds which have a lip or rim at the top edge. Glass mixing bowls and ovenproof dishes often make suitable moulds. Other

Trim the uneven edge of a papier mâché bowl with scissors

mould objects, like fresh fruit, require a different approach. When using entire shapes like these, the papier mache has to be cut away after it is dry. To do this the finished shape is cut through all round with a craft knife. The two halves are removed from the mould, and the two papier mâché shapes are joined together again with glued paper strips placed across the cut edges.

Some pieces of work like the papier mâché bangles and brooches (on page 54) and the picture frame (on page 24) are moulded over cardboard shapes. These are left in place to form a rigid base for the design.

Preparing moulds: It is necessary to lubricate the mould before applying the paper strips so that the finished papier mâché can be removed easily. Smear the mould surface liberally with petroleum jelly. If it is necessary to remove the papier mâché at any time during the drying process, re-grease the mould before replacing the work.

Working with a mould: Protect the work surface with old newspapers. When using a dish or bowl-shape moulds, invert the mould over a suitable prop like a can or mug – any object tall enough to raise the mould off the work surface and keep it stable.

Preparing paper strips: Tear paper – newspaper or copy paper – into small strips about ½in (12mm) wide × 2in (5cm) long. This size strip will mould well round most curves. (For larger or smaller projects adapt the strip size.) As a guide, the strips should adhere to the mould without pleating or distorting.

Preparing adhesive: Wallpaper paste (without fungicide) mixed to full strength is popular for working papier mâché. Drying time is slightly longer however with a very wet adhesive like this. Undiluted PVA can be added to the paste to stiffen it slightly, and to speed drying time, or you can use PVA on its own, diluted with water to a stiff cream consistency. A PVA-only solution produces papier mâché with a light, almost plastic feel to it.

Applying the strips: Starting at the top of the greased mould (the base), first use water only to dampen the strips, and smooth each one in place, overlapping edges slightly, to build a layer reaching downwards to the outside edge. Allow the strips to overlap the edge slightly, as this can be trimmed later. Apply a second layer of strips, this time using adhesive, and work the strips round the bowl in the other direction. This helps to build a firm, strong web. Paint adhesive over the surface, and smooth with your hands to remove any air bubbles. Do this after applying each layer of strips. Add another layer of glued strips, working downwards in the same direction as the first layer. Continue in this way until six or eight layers are in place. (If the bowl seems fragile when dry, you can always add more strips.) Finish with a coat of adhesive.

Drying papier mâché: Papier mâché can take several days to dry so be patient if you want successful results. Keep the mould on the prop, and leave the work to dry naturally in a warm, airy place. To hasten the process, you can place papier mâché on fireproof props in an oven, set at lowest heat. Place objects modelled all over a mould on a mesh surface such as a baking rack.

Removing work from mould: To unmould a bowl shape, gently insert a thin knife, such as a palette knife, between the bowl and the mould and slide round to break any vacuum which may have formed. Gently ease the papier mâché away, and place on work surface. Trim the uneven edge with scissors, or leave in its natural state if preferred. Check for any thin patches, and build these up with extra strips. Leave to dry. Smooth any uneven patches with sandpaper. To unmould solid shapes

(such as fruit) cut round and join with glued paper strips (see page 46).

Decorating papier mâché: Paint with a coat of white emulsion paint, or another light, opaque undercoat such as poster or acrylic paint. You can draw designs and paint on to this, or add collage decoration. Work on the inside of a bowl shape, then invert it on to a prop, and decorate the outside. If you are using

---

REMOVING GLUES

Adhesive manufacturers will always help with advice about solvents for their products and some will supply these solvents direct if you write to them. In general, the first step in glue first aid is to scrape off any deposit and then proceed as follows:

Clear adhesive:
On skin, wash first, then remove any residue with nail varnish remover. On clothing or furnishings, hold a pad of absorbent rag on the underside, dab with non-oily nail varnish remover on the right side.

Epoxy adhesive:
Lighter fuel or cellulose thinners will remove adhesive from the hands. On fabrics, hold a rag pad under the glue stain, dab with cellulose thinners on the right side. On synthetic fibres, use lighter fuel.

Adhesive tape residue:
White spirit or cellulose thinners may do it. Or try nail varnish remover. Adhesives vary and you will have to experiment.

Latex adhesive:
Lift off as much as possible before the adhesive hardens. Keep the glue soft with cold water and rub with a cloth. Treat any stains with liquid dry cleaner. Scrape off any deposits with a pencil rubber.

paints, make sure each colour is dry before proceeding to the next. Paint awkward shapes bit by bit, first painting one side and then the other, to avoid fingerprint marks. Finish by painting with one or two thin coats of varnish, applying it stage by stage. Most pieces can be left to dry on a wire rack.

To paint or varnish beads: Select a skewer or knitting needle to fit tightly through the bead, so that the bead cannot slip round. Lubricate the skewer with petroleum jelly and thread the beads on to this, leaving a gap between each one. Hold the skewer in one hand, and paint with the other. Dry by balancing the skewer between two objects, or push the end securely into pieces of modelling clay. Leave to dry.

To paint paper beads, thread them on a skewer and balance across cans

Making cardboard boxes

The boxes in this book are made in two basic ways. Boxes made from thin card are mostly made from a single sheet of card which is accurately scored along marked lines and folded into shape. Integral tabs, which are angled or curved to fit into the box without distorting it, are glued and pressed to the box sides to hold its shape. Larger boxes – too big to cut from a single sheet of card – and

With all adhesives, read the manufacturer's instructions carefully before use, and have the necessary solvents at hand to cope with accidental spills.

those made from thick card, are usually made by joining each side piece separately. Each section is glued to the other, and the sides are reinforced with gummed tape.

With most designs it is a good idea to make the box lid after the main box is covered. This is to ensure a good fit, taking into consideration the thickness of the card and the covering paper.

To make a lid, (which can often be cut from a single piece of card) take the outside measurement of each box side and mark this accurately with a set square and ruler on to the centre of a piece of card. Measure a tiny amount extra all round this shape (about $\frac{1}{8}$in (3mm) is usually enough) to allow for the thickness of the covering paper. This shape is the lid top. Extend the lines to make side pieces from this basic shape, adding tabs to each side of two sides if you are using thin card. Cut out and construct in the same way as for the box. Check the fit before gluing the lid sides, by holding them in place with a little sticky tape. For lids made piece-by-piece, measure for the lid top in the same way.

Covering boxes

Boxes can be covered with paper by adding pieces separately to each side. This is necessary for large boxes, where a single sheet may not reach all the way round. When covering a box in this way, the paper sides are cut with an overlap turning at top and base, and an overlap on each end of two sides. The other two sides are added last and are cut with side edges flush with the box sides. Corners of overlaps are trimmed diagonally to fit over edges neatly, then a base piece is fitted. Box linings are added in much the same way – just omit the top overlap. Alternatively, the box sides can be covered with one long strip and a side overlap. The finished edge is placed on to the overlap, flush with the box. The turnings for the top and base are the same, and these are snipped at each corner when fitting to the wrong side.

To cover a box, place it on the paper and draw extending lines outwards. Cut to an angle at the corners.

Glue the overlaps to the inside and ends of the box

Gift wrapping

Papercrafts lend themselves naturally to gift wrapping – box making and covering boxes, pleating paper, paper freizes and patchwork, paper flowers and lace and paper weaving. Once you have familiarized yourself with the different techniques, you can adapt your skills to creative gift wrapping.

Wrapping plain boxes is an art in itself and lovely effects can be achieved quite simply through the careful choice of paper and ribbon.

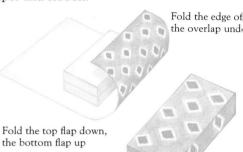

Fold the edge of the overlap unde

Fold the top flap down, the bottom flap up

Boxes
Square or rectangular box

Make sure that you have enough giftwrap paper. If necessary, tape sheets together. Use a solid glue stick (or double-sided tape) for sealing edges. Transparent adhesive tape always shows and can look messy.

Lay the box on the wrong side of the paper. Bring up the sides and then trim

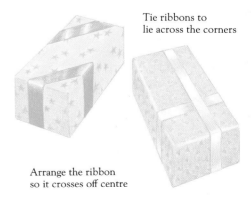

Tie ribbons to lie across the corners

Arrange the ribbon so it crosses off centre

the overlap to about 2in (5cm). Fold the edge of the overlap under. The paper should extend over the ends a little more than half the depth of the box. Glue or tape the overlap down. Fold in the sides first, then the top flap down and the bottom flap up. Glue, or fasten with a piece of double sided tape placed under the flaps so that it does not show.

Round boxes
Trace the bottom and top of the box on the wrong side of the paper. Cut out 2 circles. Measure the depth of the box and the circumference. Cut a piece of giftwrap paper to the box depth measurement plus 1in (2.5cm) with 1in (2.5cm) extra on the length for overlap. Place the paper round the box, fold under the edge of the overlap and glue. Snip into the extra paper at the top and bottom edges of the box to make tabs. Fold them in. Spread glue round the edges of the two paper circles and press them on to the tabs.

Original wraps
Although well-chosen giftwrap paper and ribbons will usually produce attractive effects, for really original packages you should treat every giftwrap as an artist treats a canvas. Look through this book and think about the things you can use as decoration, other than ribbons and bows. You could pleat cartridge paper and patterned giftwrap into miniature fans and tie them on with ribbons. Or cut shapes from white paper and prick them into paper lace with festive designs. You might make a string of paper beads with red, green and gold paper and loop them across the package. Paper flowers used singly or in posies look pretty on both summer and wintertime gifts.

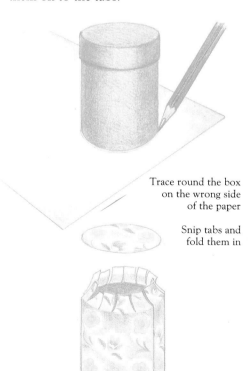

Trace round the box
on the wrong side
of the paper

Snip tabs and
fold them in

Tie on miniature
paper-fans

Loop paper beads
across the parcel

Decorate gifts with
paper flowers

Wrapping plants

Plants in pots are welcome and popular gifts and are not difficult to package attractively. You need a large sheet of stiff card, coloured on one side or with giftwrap paper laminated to it. Stand the pot in the middle of the card on the wrong side. Hold a ruler against the pot on four sides and mark the card. Join the marks and pencil the square. Remove the pot and score along the lines of the

Hold a ruler against the pot and mark the card

Ribbons and bows

Gift ribbon that sticks to itself when moistened is used to make decorative rosettes and bows. Use single colours or mix two or three shades together.

Rosette

This bow can be made with woven gift ribbon also. Loop the ribbon as shown, tie in the middle with another piece of ribbon. Spread out the loops. Fish-tail the ribbon ends.

This design can also be turned into a star by cutting each of the loops and fish-tailing the ends.

square. Next, measure the height of the pot and the plant together. Mark this measurement out from the sides of the square. Draw lines from the corners of the square to the marks. Cut out. Punch a single hole in each point about $\frac{3}{4}$in (18mm) from the tip. Stand the pot on the pencilled square, fold up the four sides and tie the box together through the punched holes with ribbon. Tie more ribbons with streamer ends to cascade down the sides of the box.

Petals

Moisten the end of a length of gift ribbon and form a small ring. Wind the ribbon round, moisten the surface and make another, slightly larger ring. Continue making rings until you have formed a petal shape. Pinch the tips. Petals can be used flat, secured to the package with double sided tape, to make a flower shape. Or several can be fastened together, points upwards, with long ribbon ends.

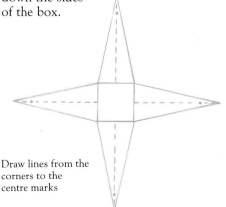

Draw lines from the corners to the centre marks

Tie ribbons through the punched holes

Flat bow

Use either gift ribbon or woven ribbon for this bow.

Cut a strip of ribbon and join both ends in the middle. Cut a short piece and bind it over the middle, joining the ends on the underside of the bow.

Make a bigger bow by cutting a long strip of ribbon and glueing down a loop at one end. Fold the ribbon to make another loop, facing the other way, glue at the centre. Continue making loops to either side of the middle, each slightly shorter than the ones before. Three or four loops is sufficient. Cut a short strip and bind the middle.

Flat bow

Daisy

Cut 4 pieces of gift ribbon about 8in (20cm) long. Lay the pieces in a star shape. Moisten and join at the centre. Bring the ends up and fasten together. Moisten the inside of the ball shape and push the top and bottom together firmly until they stick.

Chrysanthemum

Cut $\frac{1}{2}$in (12mm)-wide gift ribbon into 16in (40cm) lengths. Cut the strips down the middle. Moisten the ends of strips and join them. Turn the ring into a figure-of-eight, moisten to hold the shape. Join 2 figure-of-eights with glue. Make more figure-of-eights and add them, laying them first one way, then the other until a chrysanthemum has been formed. You will need about 14 to get the effect.

Daisy

Rosette

Petals

Chrysanthemum

STOCKISTS

Mail order suppliers of craft materials
and equipment:

Fred Aldous Ltd
P.O. Box 135
37 Lever Street
Manchester
M60 1UX

Swancraft
The Handicraft Shop
Northgate
Canterbury
CT1 1BE

Flowermaking stamens, wires and tapes:
Hamilworth Ltd
23 Lime Road
Dumbarton
Dunbartonshire
G82 2RP